Jean Ritchie's

Kentucky Mother Goose

Jean Ritchie's

Kentucky Mother Goose

Songs and Stories from My Childhood

JEAN RITCHIE with SUSAN BRUMFIELD

PICTURES BY MAURICE SENDAK

Hal Leonard Books
An Imprint of Hal Leonard Corporation

Frontispiece: Jean Ritchie with her Amburgey dulcimer at the Gatlinburg (Tennessee) Handcrafter's Fair, 1947.

Published in 2015 by Hal Leonard Books
An Imprint of Hal Leonard Corporation
7777 West Bluemound Road
Milwaukee, WI 53213

Trade Book Division Editorial Offices
33 Plymouth St., Montclair, NJ 07042

Printed in the United States of America

Book design by Damien Castaneda

Library of Congress Cataloging-in-Publication Data

Ritchie, Jean, author.
Jean Ritchie's Kentucky Mother Goose : songs and stories from my childhood / Jean Ritchie with Susan Brumfield.
pages cm
Includes bibliographical references.
ISBN 978-1-4950-0788-0
1. Ritchie, Jean--Childhood and youth. 2. Folk singers--Appalachian Region--Biography. 3. Folk songs, English--Appalachian Region. I. Brumfield, Susan, author. II. Title.
ML420.R6A3 2015
781.62'130769--dc23

2015024279

www.halleonardbooks.com

The Ritchie family, 1937. Standing: Balis (Dad), Truman, Kitty, Ray, Una, Mallie, Ollie, May, Abigail (Mom); kneeling: Jean, Wilmer, Pauline, Jewel, Edna, Patty.

I was the one in my family to get Mom and Dad started recollecting the oldest things they knew. If somebody gets really interested and starts asking questions of the older people . . . if you still have some older people around, why, please do, because they remember all kinds of things once you get them started, but you have to get 'em started.

Jean Ritchie, 1979

Contents

THREE: SCHOOLYARD PLAY AND SINGING GAMES

FOUR: JUST FOR FUN: "STRAIGHT SONGS"

Foreword

My mother learned these songs and games from her family and others in her community of Viper, Kentucky. Being the youngest of fourteen children, she was never at a loss for someone to teach her a new way to entertain herself. She and her brothers and sisters passed these treasures on to their children, and now my cousins and their children enjoy handing them down to the next generation, which continues to make our reunions lively.

In addition to the ballads, hymns, and play party and dance tunes that are a large part of the family collection, there will always be a special place for the childhood repertoire. In addition to their own folkloric value, they are also the stepping-stones that lead to a lifelong love of the music and tradition.

Jon Pickow with Jean Ritchie
January 2, 2015
Berea, Kentucky

Jean Ritchie and Jon Pickow, Hindman Settlement School, 2006.

Preface

When Jean Ritchie's *Singing Family of the Cumberlands* made its first appearance in print in 1955, it earned high praise from readers and reviewers alike. Jean had originally envisioned the book as an anthology, with a few introductory remarks for each song. But her publishers, impressed with her writing style, suggested that she narrow the number of songs and focus instead on her story. The result was a family biography, described in the *Chicago Sunday Tribune* as "one of the most appealing accounts of family life in a long time . . . an important bit of Americana." A reviewer for the *New York Herald Tribune Book Review* wrote, "She writes as she sings—naturally and with an instinctive sense for rhythms." In the *Kentucky Folklore Journal*, William H. Jansen observed that Jean "somehow made her style perfectly natural, the only appropriate vehicle for her story. No greater compliment could be paid to a prose writer." Twenty-five years later, noted Kentucky folklorist Loyal Jones revisited *Singing Family* in an article for the 1981 *Appalachian Journal*, describing Jean's writing as "both witty and profound." In his words, the book "tells you who she is, and how she knows who she is."

"Who she is" today, at the age of 92, is an extraordinary individual who has been a collector, keeper, and champion of her family's treasured repertory for most of her life. Jean Ritchie is an internationally acclaimed singer, songwriter, and dulcimer player whose concert and recording career has spanned more than seven decades. She has inspired documentaries and dissertations, and most recently, a tribute album; *Dear Jean: Artists Celebrate Jean Ritchie* is a beautiful compilation of her songs, performed by some of today's finest artists in traditional music. She has written ten books (this is her eleventh) and numerous articles, and has presented master classes and lectures for performers, academics, and music educators throughout the country. She holds two honorary doctorates and was named as a 2002 National Heritage Fellow by the

Jean teaching singing games to students at New York's Henry Street Settlement School, ca. 1947.

National Endowment for the Arts. Though Jean Ritchie is best known as a performer, her work as a folk song collector, author, and educator deserves equal recognition.

The reputation of the Ritchies as a "singing family" is well documented; Jean, born in 1922 as the youngest of fourteen children, grew up making music in and around her home in Viper, Kentucky. While still in school, she started gathering songs from her immediate and extended family. By the time she left home in 1946 (as a Phi Beta Kappa graduate of the University of Kentucky) to become a social worker at the Henry Street Settlement School in New York, Jean had already amassed a repertoire of more than 300 songs.

As part of her work at the Henry Street Settlement, Jean taught songs and games to children there in the Lower East Side. Her subsequent acquaintance with folklorist Alan Lomax led to his recording her Kentucky songs for the Library of Congress's Archive of American Folk Song (now the Archive of Folk Culture). Jean gradually began making a place for herself on the folk scene, giving concert appearances in New York and at festivals, folk clubs, and college campuses across the country. She performed regularly on radio and television and enjoyed an active recording career. In 1950, Jean married photographer and filmmaker George Pickow, and the following year, she was awarded a Fulbright grant to research the roots of her own family's music, and to learn more about the culture from which it came. Jean and George spent fourteen months during 1952–53 traveling throughout England, Ireland, and Scotland, documenting their folk song collecting with recordings and photographs. While in the U.K., Jean also performed concerts in major venues as part of the growing folk revival.

I had an opportunity to work with Jean directly while investigating her work in Scotland (the topic of my dissertation). During visits to their home in Port Washington, she and George opened the book on a fascinating chapter in their lives and their groundbreaking fieldwork. Jean introduced me to Hamish Henderson, the folklorist, scholar, philosopher, poet, and musician extraordinaire whose recollections of their joint ventures in Scotland brought the folk music revival to life before my eyes (and ears). One of the many facets of Hamish's collection involved children's singing games; he and Alan Lomax (and later, Kenneth Goldstein) made recordings in streets and playgrounds in the 1950s (as did collector James T. R. Ritchie). I knew that as soon as my study on Ms. Ritchie's fieldwork was complete, I would return to Scotland to dig into those recordings. Many return visits and subsequent research there culminated in a scholarly anthology for music teachers, *Hot Peas and Barley-O: Children's Songs and Games from Scotland.*

Jean was a regular advisor on that project; she guided me toward archives, arranged professional introductions on my behalf, and helped with historical research, once even calling upon her loyal "Mud-catters" to help trace the roots of an elusive harvest custom song. (For several years, Jean was a regular contributor and correspondent in online folk music forums in the Mudcat Café, commenting modestly—and mostly anonymously—under the name "Kytrad." Many of the online threads still contain lively conversations and words of wisdom from Jean's experience as both collector and performer.) She offered advice for the teachers who wanted to incorporate folk music into the classroom:

> *I would urge them to try to hear the real music, instead of just the "prettied-up" thing. There's a place for that too, I suppose. But if they want to use the songs with children, for educational purposes, they need to hear how the people really sounded back then; how the people really sang.*

I came to realize that this kind of generosity is a hallmark characteristic of Jean Ritchie. A true celebrity in folk music circles, Jean is quick to compliment and support the efforts of aspiring musicians and scholars; she always finds a kind word of praise for others. When I asked her if she would write a few words for my book, she graciously penned a beautiful foreword:

> *. . . We all remember what we played and sang in our younger days, and when we open these pages, we're right back in those times. The words and tunes are a bit different, but the same happy feelings of excitement, joy and the never-ending-ness of childhood shine through. Almost every title in this collection reminds me immediately of "the way we played it" or "the way our song went" in the Kentucky Mountains.*

In her closing remarks, Jean wrote, ". . . The next thing I'm inspired to do is to recollect and write down all my memories of our childhood songs and games. Perhaps all of you will do the same." That was the first step toward our collaboration on *Jean Ritchie's Kentucky Mother Goose.*

Jean and George came to Texas twice during the next several years. In 2005, she gave a series of workshops at Texas Tech University culminating in an event called "A Tribute to Jean Ritchie." At age 82, Jean presented sessions for music teachers, university students, and academic scholars; for two full days, she taught singing games, lectured on her fieldwork, and brought down the house in a stunning concert performance of her music. She later made a return appearance at the OAKE National Conference, this time in San Antonio. By then, our plans for her *Kentucky Mother Goose* were taking shape.

We tossed ideas back and forth via email and phone conversations; in the meantime, Jean made lists of all the songs she could remember, and notes about when, where, and from whom she had learned them. I began compiling background information from Jean's earlier publications, liner notes from her recordings, and from her own recollections. We spent several days in Port Washington in November 2007, working together on the project. As always, George was in and out, offering suggestions and reminding Jean of photos and recordings we might want to include.

I worked my way through Jean's handwritten notes, transcribing tunes as she sang them for me. Though a bit under the weather, Jean was cheerful, patiently answering endless questions about one song or another. As our time was running out, she agreed to record the songs we hadn't gotten to for me, "just so you can get them down right." She'd had a cold and didn't feel as though she sounded her best, but to my ears, her voice was as beautiful and true as ever. Jean's son Jon set us up in their home studio; Jean sang fragments and we chatted and laughed about the songs. How I wish we had recorded them all!

Just before her eighty-seventh birthday in December of 2009, Jean suffered a serious stroke. She was hospitalized, and later, transferred to a rehabilitation facility, but after several months of steady and remarkable improvement, she was able to return to her home, where she was able to be with her husband until his death the following December.

In 2011, Jean moved back to Kentucky, where she now resides near close family and friends in Berea. When she was well enough to enjoy spending time with visitors, I planned a trip to see her. I brought along photos and recordings of our concerts and workshops together, and presented her with a (very) rough draft of our manuscript. To my delight, Jean showed interest in completing her *Kentucky Mother Goose*, and since then, her family, friends, and devoted fans have all pitched in to help gather additional material for the book. Jean herself has been involved in the final stages of its preparation, identifying family photos, making corrections in my notation, and singing through the songs along with me. In fact, during a recent visit to Berea, I received a lesson in the finer points of playing "club fist"!

It has been nearly ten years since Jean and I began work on *Kentucky Mother Goose*. In gathering and compiling material from more than sixty years of Jean's written work and spoken interviews, I have become aware of the striking element of consistency in Jean's message: It is always her voice which comes through, quiet but clear, and it has always been her intention to honor her music, her family, and the tradition of which they are a part. In a 1979 concert at Berea College, Jean reflected on writing *Singing Family of the Cumberlands* ("It took a few years"). She said that she wanted to write about the songs and talk about each one, telling "where it fit in the family and who sang it." As an academic scholar and expert, Jean is well informed in the historical roots of her songs, but in the past, her approach has been to focus instead on presenting them in their "proper family setting." It is in the spirit of that intention that we present this book.

Susan Brumfield
January 5, 2015

Note: Jean Ritchie passed away peacefully on the first of June, 2015, shortly after the last draft of her *Kentucky Mother Goose* was completed. She spent her last days at home in Berea, surrounded by dear family members who filled the hours at her bedside singing their beloved Ritchie family songs. Jean was laid to rest beside her husband, George Pickow, in the beautiful hilltop cemetery near her family home in Viper, Kentucky.

Acknowledgments

My sincere thanks go to the Ritchie family of Kentucky for their generosity in sharing not only their songs, but also their rich family history, told through Jean's recollections. In particular, I wish to thank Jean's niece, Judy Ritchie Hudson, and Judy's husband, Frank Hudson, for their kind hospitality and assistance during my visits to Jean's home in Berea. Frank was also extremely helpful in gathering rare family photographs; he scanned, digitized, and shared images, including photos taken by George Pickow, and snapshots and prints from Jean Ritchie's personal collection and from his own work as a photographer. I am deeply grateful to Jean's sons, Jon and Peter Pickow, for their support of this "labor of love." Jon has been involved in Jean's *Kentucky Mother Goose* project since its inception, engineering the 2007 recordings of Jean and offering creative suggestions and feedback as the project unfolded. Peter handled contractual details on Jean's behalf, and ensured that permission to include her copyrighted material was granted.

I would like to acknowledge the archivists, librarians, and institutions that allowed me to work with the sound recordings, photographs, and print material used in the book. I owe a debt of gratitude to Dr. Ron Pen, director of the John Jacob Niles Center for American Music at the University of Kentucky, without whose help I might never have met Jean Ritchie. A longtime friend of Jean and her family, Ron wrote the foreword to the 1996 edition of her *Folk Songs of the Southern Appalachians*. During the early stages of my dissertation research (on Jean's 1951–52 fieldwork in Scotland), I contacted Ron to ask for help. He immediately put me in touch with Ms. Ritchie at home in Port Washington, New York, opening the door for my ongoing association and friendship with her. When the opportunity to compile this anthology arose years later, Ron graciously met with me at the

Niles Center, offering encouragement and advice. Additionally, Gordon Hogg, Special Collections Library director at UK, and Matt Harris, research and reference coordinator, hastily arranged a visit to the library for me during a brief stop in Lexington and provided access to Jean's papers there, including the original typescript of her first book, *Singing Family of the Cumberlands.*

I would like to thank Nathan Salsburg, curator of the Alan Lomax Archive at the Association for Cultural Equity, for facilitating the process by which permission to include Alan Lomax's 1949 archival recordings of Ms. Ritchie was granted, and for helping us to quickly procure digital masters of the tapes. Thanks also to Harry Rice, sound archivist at Berea College, for guiding me to the Ritchie family photographs and to Jean Ritchie's sound and video recordings in the Hutchins Library Special Collections & Archives. I am also grateful to Marcia Segal and Todd Harvey, archivists at the American Folklife Center at the Library of Congress, and to Michael Wu for his assistance with archival research there.

It is an exceptional delight to include rare and previously unseen drawings by Maurice Sendak in *Jean Ritchie's Kentucky Mother Goose.* Mr. Sendak was the illustra-

Jean Ritchie with her dulcimer, early 1950s.

tor for 1955's *Singing Family*, and these four unpublished sketches were discovered among the original drawings used in that book. Kind thanks to Mrs. Iona Opie for aid in tracking down the illustrations; and also to Justin C. Schiller of Battledore Press, for solving the mystery of their disappearance (and reappearance some thirty years later). I am deeply indebted to Patrick Rodgers, of The Rosenbach Museum & Library in Philadelphia, for providing access to the drawings. Special thanks are owed to The Maurice Sendak Foundation, Inc., with whose kind permission we were able to include the drawings.

I would like to acknowledge several individuals who stepped in to provide logistical assistance, tie up loose ends, and gather material needed to "fill in the gaps." Steve Shaffer, staff photographer for Kentucky Educational Television, tracked down negatives of Ritchie family photographs used in the making of the documentary *Mountain Born: The Jean Ritchie Story*. Steve hand-delivered the negatives to Murphy's Camera in Lexington, where the staff swiftly digitized prints and expedited their delivery to me in Texas. Mack McCormick at The University Press of Kentucky clarified facts and supplied important documentation pertaining to the copyright of Ms. Ritchie's previously published material.

Among Jean's countless admirers and friends, two in particular—Mick Lane and Dan Schatz—offered help on a moment's notice. Along with Charlie Pilzer, Mick and Dan coproduced *Dear Jean: Artists Celebrate Jean Ritchie*. The two-CD recording, which has received critical acclaim and risen to the top of the folk music charts, pays tribute to Jean with performances of her music by such luminaries as Judy Collins, Oscar Brand, Kathy Mattea, Janis Ian, John McCutcheon, and others. The album also includes a spoken-word piece by Pete Seeger (one of his last recordings), along with cuts by "up-and-coming" traditional performers and members of the Ritchie family. Dan kindly shared invaluable finding aids and additional photographs gleaned from the hours he spent poring through the Ritchie-Pickow papers in the Library of

Jean Ritchie and Susan Brumfield perform "Jemmy Taylor-O" at the "Tribute to Jean Ritchie" concert at Texas Tech University, Lubbock, Texas, 2005.

Members of the Ritchie family at the graduation of Jean's sister Kitty from Berea College, circa 1939. Left to right: Jean's sister Patty, parents Balis and Abigail, and siblings Wilmer, Pauline, Jewel, Edna, and Ollie Mae.

Congress Folk Music Archive, preparing liner notes for the CD.

Numerous family and extended family members, who gathered in Viper for the 2015 Ritchie Family Reunion, shared stories and provided background for many of the photos in the book. One particular mystery involved tracking down an unidentified woman pictured with Jean, and thanks to clues from Raymond McLain, director at the Kentucky Center for Traditional Music at Morehead State University, and David Brose, archivist at the John C. Campbell Folk School, we were able to redirect our search. Cathy Hendrix, an avid collector and expert on contemporary American folk art, and artist A. Jann Peitso were able to locate several informants in Gatlinburg, Tennessee (including the brother of our "mystery lady"), who immediately identified her as the late Lucinda Oakley Ogle, descendant of a prominent Smoky Mountain family, storyteller, and author. I am grateful to both for their tenacity and skillful sleuthing.

Gifted photographer, exquisite singer, and native Kentuckian Jeannie Lovett Barrick consolidated, edited, and prepared the photos for publication. Jeannie's deep Kentucky musical roots lent unique insight into the book and its accompanying images; I cherish her fond affection for the work, and appreciate her generous and valuable contribution to it. I owe very special thanks to Donna Hogan Devane, former Texas Tech University research assistant, now a freelance editor of academic and educational publications, for devoting time to this project during a particularly full production schedule. As always, I relied on Donna's resourceful fact-checking, editorial expertise, and meticulous attention to detail while preparing the final draft of the material. I also wish to thank Michael Konczal for his helpful advice and thoughtful perspective.

I am profoundly thankful for the musical and technical expertise of Professor Will

Women quilting in the Ritchie family home in 1950, before Jean's September wedding to George Pickow. Jean is in front, second from left, with her back to the camera, and Jean's mother, Abigail, is at upper right.

Strieder, my extraordinary university colleague, friend, and longtime collaborator on educational publications and recordings. Will painstakingly preserved, restored, and remastered snippets of voice memos and rough interview recordings, and compiled them, along with various home studio recordings, archival tapes, and early commercial recordings, so that the songs in the book might come to life in Jean's own voice.

Jean, with Susan Brumfield, at Jean's home in Berea, Kentucky, 2012.

I cannot imagine undertaking this project (or any other publication) without the ongoing guidance and support of the creative and visionary leadership at the Hal Leonard Corporation. Sincere thanks to Emily Crocker, vice president of choral publications, Bruce Bush, sales and marketing manager for educational publications, and especially to Myra Murray, with whom I have had the pleasure of collaborating on two previous anthologies, *Hot Peas and Barley-O: Children's Songs and Games from Scotland* and *Over the Garden Wall: Children's Songs and Games from England*, as well as the *First, We Sing!* series of Kodály-inspired materials for classroom music teachers. I am grateful to Myra, Bruce, and Emily for steering this project into the hands of John Cerullo, group publisher at Hal Leonard Performing Arts Publishing Group. This book would not have come to fruition without John's kind and patient guidance, his savvy knowledge of the industry, and his willingness to coordinate the complex pieces of this very special project. I also wish to thank project editor Jessica Burr and copy editor Josh Wimmer for their editorial guidance and careful preparation of the manuscript.

Finally, this book is dedicated to Jean Ritchie Pickow, and to the memory of her husband, George Pickow. It has been a blessing, an honor, and a great privilege to have a hand in bringing Jean's marvelous warmth, wit, and charm to the "wider world," along with the music and stories of her Kentucky childhood.

M. Sendak

ONE

Songs at Home

CHURNING SONG

Churning chant

Ritchie family version

Jean's mother, Abigail Hall Ritchie, churns butter while Jean's father, Balis Ritchie, plays a tune and looks on.

Jean recalled that once, when she was a little girl, her older sisters decided to tease her by locking the old screen door to the kitchen, pretending they couldn't see her or hear her knocking to get in. She begged, cried, and banged her fists on the door, but they kept right on singing and getting the dinner up. Finally, little Jean picked up a broom handle and ran it right through the screen door! The girls laughed, and Jean's mother (Abigail Ritchie) laughed, too, but she decided that her little "bad girl" would have to finish churning the butter that night.

Jean tried her hardest, but the paddle was heavy, and the churn was full. Finally, Abigail drew the little crying girl into her lap and held her as they churned together. Jean said, "She wiped my tears with my dress tail and ran her hands, cool from being outdoors, over my hot, wet, miserable face and settled me in the big crook of her left arm, giving me a secret hug . . . we churned. I 'snubbed' once in a while, but Mommy kept talking to the time of the churning and my heart began to ease." Her mother said, "There, now, don't you cry, hush your cryin' by and by, then we'll make the butter fly, Mommy's baby, don't you cry . . ."

DARBY'S LAMB (THE DARBY RAM)

Abigail Ritchie version

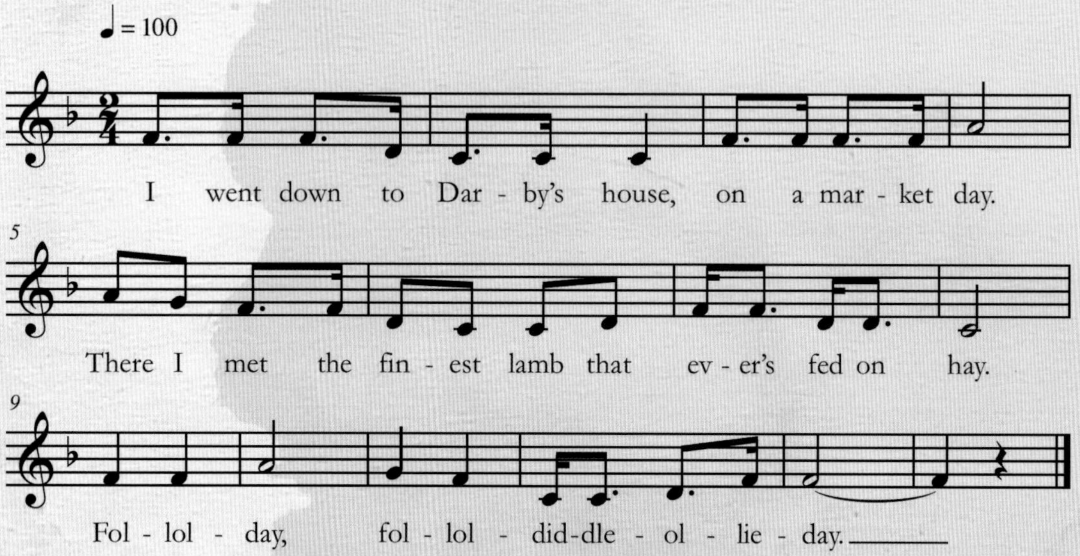

2. The first tooth he had held a hundred of a horn.
The next tooth he had held sixty barrel o' corn.
Fol-lol-day, fol-lol-diddle-ollie-day.

3. Four feet he had; four feet stood on the ground.
And every foot that he had covered a half an acre of ground.
Fol-lol-day, fol-lol-diddle-ollie-day.

4. The wool on the lamb's bell drug nine miles on the ground.
I went down to Darby's house and stole a thousand pound.
Fol-lol-day, fol-lol-diddle-ollie-day.

5. The wool on the lamb's back, it reached up to the sky.
The eagles built their nests there, you could hear the young 'un cry.
Fol-lol-day, fol-lol-diddle-ollie-day.

6. The one that cut his throat got drownded in the blood.
The one that held his head got washed away in the flood.
O, fol-lol-day, fol-lol-diddle-ollie-day.

Abigail Hall Ritchie learned this song from her mother, Patty, who died when Abigail was still a young child. Jean calls it "Grandmother Hall's lullaby song," and remembers her mother singing it, too. Telling me about this song, Jean laughingly recalled that her mother called it "Darby's Lamb," "You know, because the ladies were very shy about . . . talking about . . . rams."

Jean stitches a quilt with her mother, Abigail Hall Ritchie.

GOD BLESS THE MOON

I see the moon and the moon sees me.
The moon sees the somebody I want to see.
God bless the moon, and God bless me,
And God bless the somebody I want to see.

The Ritchie-Pickow cabin, near Viper, Kentucky.

Jean sings this song on the album *Jean Ritchie at Home*. In the album's liner notes, she describes singing it as a child:

> *When the moon is new, it comes up early on a summer's evening, before dark, and before your friends go home to supper. We'd be playing "Five-ten," "Froggie in the Meadow," "Anty-Over," "London's Bridge," and games like that. Sometimes, as the little moon rim brightened and the twilight softened, we girls would link arms and walk around the yard and garden singing this song to the new moon. We never thought a thing about why we did that, but after I grew up, I read in an old book that little girls have been doing it just so, for hundreds of years!*

Balis Ritchie and Abigail Hall Ritchie with baby Jean, 1924.

HUSH, LITTLE BABY

Balis Ritchie version

If that weddin' ring don't shine,
Poppy's gonna get you a hook and a line.
If that hook and line gets broke,
Poppy's gonna get you a nanny goat.
If that nanny goat should go dry,
Poppy's gonna get you a butterfly.
If that butterfly fly away,
Poppy's gonna rock his baby all day.

Jean's father, Balis Ritchie, was a stern and quiet man. In telling me about his version of this well-known song, Jean recalled that her "first discovery about Dad was that he was a fine singer." She said, "I soon found out that Dad had hundreds of songs from his growing days, old story ballads, love songs, fun songs, dancy songs, that he never used to sing for any of us children, because we didn't know he knew them."

A handwritten caption on the back of this photo reads, "Playin' at the branch at Viper."

SWING-A-SWONG

Abigail Ritchie version

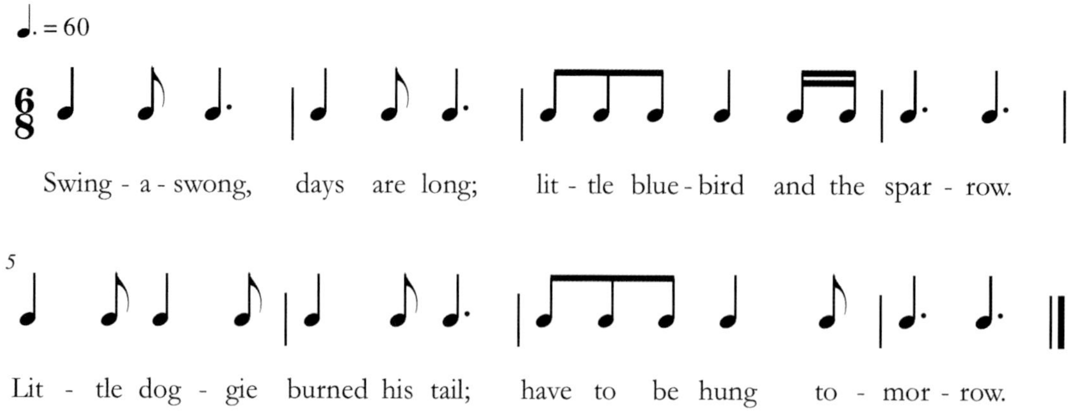

Jean, wearing a smocked blouse handmade by older sister Mallie. The house (at the mouth of the holler in Viper) belonged to her uncle Philip Hall, Abigail Hall's brother.

In *Singing Family of the Cumberlands*, Jean writes about "the summer twilights, when the song and tale-telling moved out onto the front porch." She says, "Even before I was old enough to take much part in anything else the grownups did, I was doing my share of singing the moon up on those soft summer nights." Her favorite place on the porch was the swing, "in between Mom and whatever sister got there" after she did. "I loved the lazy motion of the old swing and the way it creaked in time to the music, fast little squawks with the quick tunes, melancholy moans with the slow sad ones."

Jean recalls, "Just sitting in the swing with Mom, the swing chains would go 'screak, screak, screak, screak.' And while that was going on, she would just chant this little thing to me."

The Hall house at Mace's Creek.

TWO

Counting-Out and Other Rhymes

A GUESSING GAME

Riddle t'ma riddle t'ma riddle't'ma-ree.
I see something that you don't see.
And it's RED.

A MAN OF WORDS AND NOT OF DEEDS

A man of words and not of deeds
Is like a garden full of seeds.
When the seeds begin to grow,
Like a garden full of snow.
When the snow begins to melt,
Like a garden full of hemp.
When the hemp becomes a rope,
Like a garden full of hope.
When the rope begins to crack,
Like a hickory 'round your back.
When your back begins to smart,
Like a penknife in your heart—
And sure, in your deeds, you're *out*!

The roots of this rhyme are found in print as far back as 1899, in Percy B. Green's *A History of Nursery Rhymes*. Jean "filled in" the Kentucky verses with her own rhyming couplets. The original text is below:

A man of words and not of deeds
Is like a garden full of weeds.
And when the weeds begin to grow,
It's like a garden full of snow.
And when the snow begins to fall,
It's like a bird upon the wall.
And when the bird away does fly,
It's like an eagle in the sky.
And when the sky begins to roar,
It's like a lion at the door.
And when the door begins to crack,

It's like a stick across your back.
And when your back begins to smart,
It's like a penknife in your heart.
And when your heart begins to bleed,
You're dead, and dead, and dead indeed.

BLINDMAN'S BLUFF

Mommie and Daddy want you.
What for?
Stir the mush.
Where's the spoon?
Over this wide room.

"It" is blindfolded and turned round several times. At "over this wide room," "it" is shoved forward. He tries to tag and identify others, and the last one to be caught is "it" for the next game.

Jean, with childhood friends from Viper. The original caption reads: "Steve and Cynthia Stephenson, and David and Sally and Jean Ritchie [center]. Steve and Cynthia lived opposite Chittenden (across the main road, in the big house)."

FROGGY IN THE MEADOW

Jean taught this game to me in 2005. She explained:

> *It's not really a song; it's a chant. I think they circled around, and they kept their eyes shut. They weren't supposed to watch where he went. And he could hide, but he didn't have to; if there wasn't any place to hide, he would get behind somebody or something like that. The chant was almost a tune, but it was always the same. They'd walk around in a circle, but he's in the middle. But as soon as they start to sing, he ducks out and hides himself. And they'd sing:*

Froggy in the meadow; can't get out!
Take a little stick and stir him all about!
Kick him 'bout, kick him 'bout! Froggy's gone.
Where's Froggy?

> *And that was almost a tune, you know, but it was always the same. And when they said "stir him all about," they would go in with their arms and try to hit him, if he was in there. And when they said "kick him 'bout," they'd kick into the middle, all with their eyes closed. But they kicked first one foot, and then the other, and they would kick each other sometimes. If he hadn't gone, they'd kick him!*

JEAN, JEAN HAD A MACHINE

Name game

Jean, Jean had a machine.
Joe, Joe made it go.
Frank, Frank turned the crank.
Mommie came out and gave them a spank,
And they all rolled over the riverbank.

GEORGIE BUM-BORGIE

Name game

Georgie bum-borgie te-orgie go-forgie,
Tee-legged, tie-legged, bow-legged Georgie!
Jean bum-bean te-ean, go-fean,
Tee-legged, tie-legged, bow-legged Jean!

JAYBIRD, JAYBIRD, SITTIN' ON A LIMB

Jaybird, Jaybird, sittin' on a limb,
He winked at me, and I winked at him.
Jaybird, Jaybird, sittin' on a rail,
Middle-moddle went his head—*flip* went his tail!

Portrait of Jean on a foot-log over a creek, near Viper, Kentucky.

TAKE IT OFF OR KNOCK IT OFF

Jean taught me how to play "club fist" during my visit to her home in Berea, Kentucky, in October 2014. As she described it, one player—the leader—puts his fist on the table with his thumb sticking up. A second player grabs onto the sticking-up thumb with *his* thumb up, and the others follow. The leader says to the top thumb's owner, "Take it off or knock it off?" The owner answers with either "Take it off" (and does so) or "Knock it off." If "Knock it off" is the reply, the leader hits the owner's hand until he knocks it loose, and the player is then out. The game continues until all are out, except for the last player. The leader begins the following dialogue with the remaining player:

Jean and Susan playing "club fist" in Berea, Kentucky, 2014.

"What you got in there?"
"Pot of gold."
"Where's my part?"
"In the woods."
"Where's the woods?"
"Fire burnt it."
"Where's the fire?"
"Water squenched it."
"Where's the water?"
"Ox drunk it."
"Where's the ox?"
"Ax killed him."
"Where's the ax?"
"Hammer broke it."
"Where's the hammer?"
"Behind Granny's kitchen door, crackin' hickory nuts."

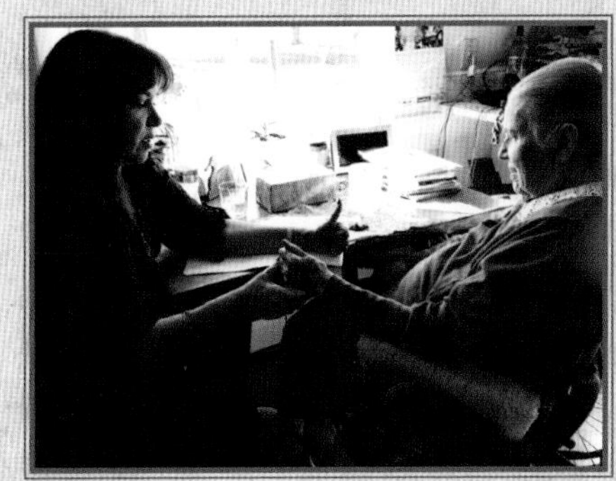

"Take it off . . ."

"And the first one to smile or show his teeth will get a hammer on the head and ten little red nails." (A closed fist hammers the head; the little red nails are pinches!)

". . . or knock it off!"

TROT-A-LITTLE HORSIE

Trot-a-little horsie, go downtown,
Don't mind, little horse, you fall down.
Little girl fell, stumped her toe,
Found her a little boy, his name was Joe.

Jean Ritchie Lane, on the road to Jean's cabin. Slabtown Hollow near Viper, Kentucky.

WILLIAM TREMMYTOE

Jean calls this a "Kentucky counting-out rhyme," but it was also once popular in the U.K. and throughout the United States. An African-American version from the Georgia Sea Islands, called "William William Trembletoe," appears in Bessie Jones and Bess Lomax Hawes's *Step It Down*, along with Mrs. Jones's description of the play, which is nearly identical to the way Jean played it in Kentucky. In Jean's version, each of the children places an index finger on the counter's knee, making a ring of fingers.

As the counter touches each finger on the beat of the rhyme, he chants:

William Tremmytoe, he's a good waterman,
Catches hens, puts 'em in pens.
Some lay eggs, some none.
Wire, briar, limber-lock,
Three geese in a flock.
One flew east, one flew west,
One flew over the cuckoo's nest.
Three little hully-gulls sitting in the spring,
O-U-T spells out you go, you old dirty dishrag, YOU!

Jean, teaching "William Tremmytoe" to a group of girls, including great-nieces Brittany and Ashley Hudson (second and fourth from left).

M. Sendak

THREE

Schoolyard Play and Singing Games

AMONG THE LITTLE WHITE DAISIES

Singing game
Ritchie family version

2. Robinson is her second name,
   Second name, second name.
   Robinson is her second name,
   Among the little white daisies.

3. Peter is his first name,
   First name, first name.
   Peter is his first name,
   Among the little white daisies.

4. Ritchie is his second name,
   Second name, second name.
   Ritchie is his second name,
   Among the little white daisies.

5. Now poor Peter is dead and gone,
   Dead and gone, dead and gone.
   Now poor Peter is dead and gone,
   Among the little white daisies.

6. Left poor Jeannie a widow now,
   Widow now, widow now.
   Left poor Jeannie a widow now,
   Among the little white daisies.

7. Twenty-four children at her feet,
At her feet, at her feet.
Twenty-four children at her feet,
Among the little white daisies.

This song appears in Jean's 1957 recording *Children's Songs and Games from the Southern Mountains*. Jean also included the song in her 1965 anthology *Folk Songs of the Southern Appalachians*. Both sources provide these instructions for the game:

During the first two verses, a circle of children revolves about a child in the center. The center child names a sweetheart, and the line changes directions and revolves the other way for the next two stanzas. For stanza five, the children put their heads on their hands (pretending to be dead). In stanza six, everyone cries in sorrow for the widow (or widower). At the end of the last stanza, the children in the circle kneel, and the center child (the widow) counts heads 'round the circle to twenty-four. The twenty-fourth child is "it" for the next round.

The "little white daisies" of Jean's Kentucky variant are "lily-white daisies" in an 1886 version from Washington, D.C., reported by William Wells Newell. In their book *The Singing Game*, Iona and Peter Opie link the text and tune (along with the singing game itself) to the Scottish "wedding ring game" "Merry-ma-Tansy," which dates back to the early seventeenth century.

Jean's sister Edna Ritchie Baker, bookmobile driver, playing dulcimer for children at Home Place, near Ary, Kentucky, ca. 1949.

CHICK-TO-MA, CHICK-TO-MA CRANIE CROW

Chase game

Ritchie family version

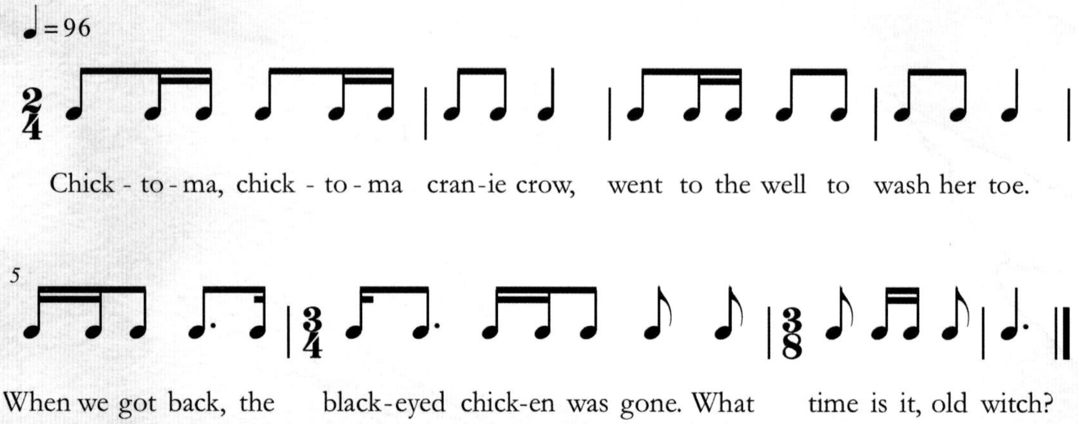

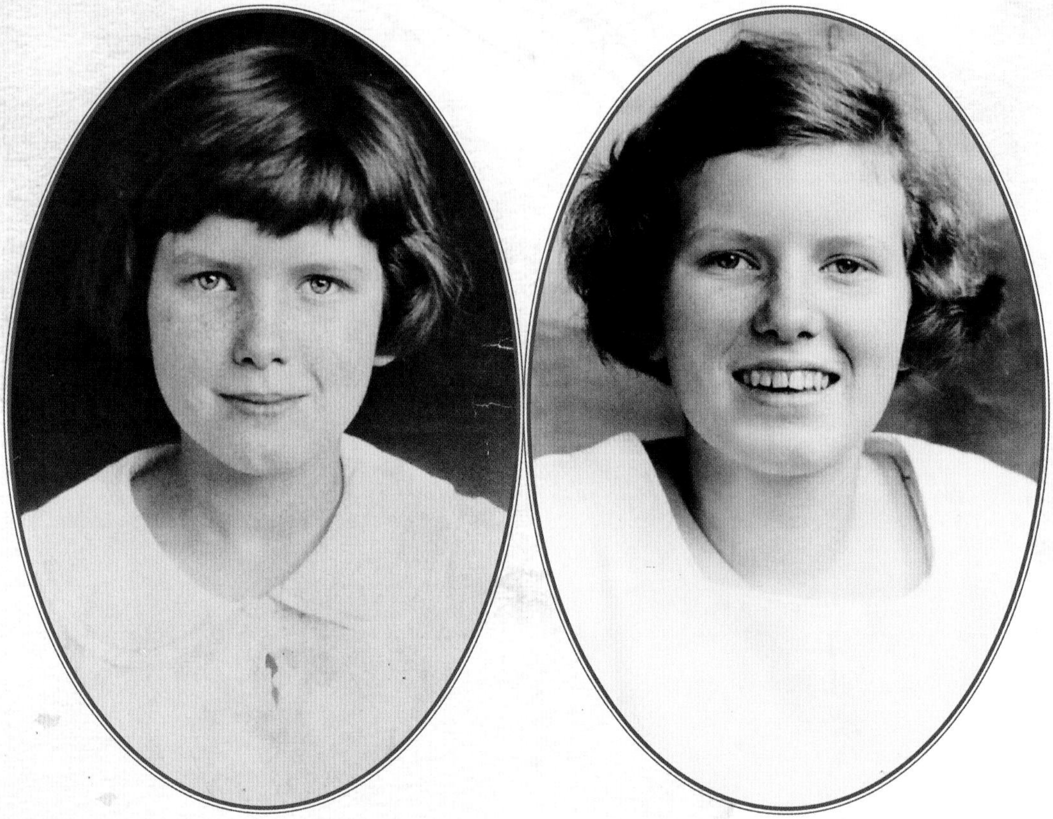

School pictures of Jean, circa 1932 (left) and 1936.

This "chase game" is best described in Jean's own words.

> *Here's a game called "Chick-to-ma-cranie-crow," and it's got a ritual thing. It's a tag game, and this is from the family, from Mom and from all the people, and this is the way it went. And again, not a tune, but just a chant:*

Chick-to-ma, chick-to-ma cranie crow,
Went to the well to wash her toe,
When we got back, the black-eyed chicken was gone.
What time is it, old witch? (Six o'clock.)
Chick-to-ma, chick-to-ma cranie crow . . .

> *And over and over again like that until she said, "Twelve o'clock."*
>
> *They would march in a line toward the others who were standing in their circle, you know, and back and forth. And then, "What time is it, old witch?" . . . They are up pretty close to her circle, and then she gives the time, the "six o'clock," and they know that that's not it, and they keep marching a little closer. She tries to get 'em as close as possible before she says "twelve o'clock," and then leaps forward and tries to catch 'em. And then everybody had to run, because she'd try to tag everybody, that was, until they got back to their home. The ones she tagged were on her side and tried to catch the others, until one side was bankrupt and won the game.*

GO IN AND OUT THE WINDOW

Singing game
Ritchie family version

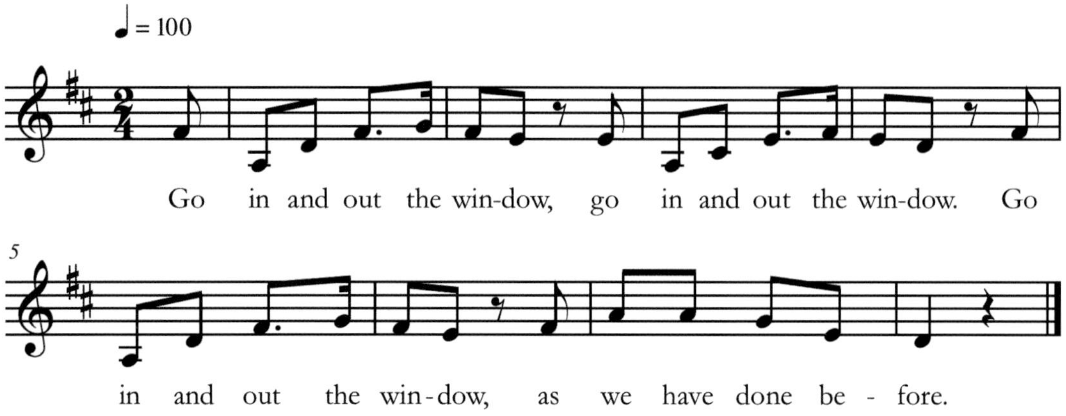

2. Stand forth and face your lover,
   Stand forth and face your lover.
   Stand forth and face your lover,
   As we have done before.

3. I kneel because I love you,
   I kneel because I love you.
   I kneel because I love you,
   As we have done before.

4. I'll measure my love to show you,
   I'll measure my love to show you.
   I'll measure my love to show you,
   As we have done before.

5. I'll break my neck to kiss you,
   I'll break my neck to kiss you.
   I'll break my neck to kiss you,
   As we have done before.

Jean recorded "Go In and Out the Window" for the 1957 album *Children's Songs and Games from the Southern Mountains.* In our interview, she recalled it as one of the favorite games at school, where children played in the yard outside the two-room schoolhouse near Viper.

In the liner notes of the album, Jean gives these instructions for the game:

> *A circle of children is formed, with hands joined, and facing the center. When the singing begins, a child in the center of the circle weaves in and out under the arches. On the second stanza, the child chooses a partner and faces him or her. On the third stanza, the child in the middle kneels before the chosen partner. On the fourth stanza, the partners hold hands, stretching out their arms and making a windmill motion with their arms going back and forth. On the fifth stanza, the center child chases his partner through the arches until he catches and kisses her! The game begins again with the chosen partner becoming the person in the center.*

Schoolhouse at Viper, Kentucky.

GOLDEN RING AROUND THE SUSAN GIRL

Play-party game
Ritchie family version

3. Do-si-do left, you Susan girl.
4. Do-si-do right, you Susan girl.
5. Hand over hand, you Susan girl.
6. Get a little faster, Susan girl.
7. Then take 'im on home, Susan girl.

"Golden Ring Around the Susan Girl" always makes me smile, because I still hear Jean's voice in my head, calling me "Susan Girl," after the song. Jean told me that she learned the play-party at school when she was about six years old. A little girl named Hazel had gathered a group together and shown them how to play, and later, Jean had learned more verses at home from her sisters Edna and Patty.

Jean's sister Edna Ritchie plays accordion with a group of girls.

GREEN GRAVEL

Singing game
Ritchie family version

Jean described her version of "Green Gravel" to me as having "an old tune to it," and its melody does differ from more commonly known versions. She said, "It's a schoolyard game we always played with the kids, with our friends." It also appears on her recording *Children's Songs and Games from the Southern Mountains.*

> Green gravel, green gravel, the grass is so green.
> All over creation, ashamed to be seen.
> Oh, Jenny, oh Jenny, your true love is dead.
> He wrote you a letter to turn back your head.

"They're all walking in a circle; just strolling in a circle and singing that, and when Jenny is named, she turns around and walks in the circle facing outward. And they do that until they get everybody turned outward. And then they start going around very fast in an outward thing, which is very hard to do, and pretty soon it breaks."

I asked, "And they do it 'til they fall down and break? Do they say anything when they go around backwards fast?"

Jean laughed and replied, "No, they just laugh. They just laugh and go, 'Hee!!!!' And then finally it breaks and they all fall down, and that's the end. It's just fun. It's no point to it. It's just . . . hearing their names called is exciting."

JENNY, PUT YOUR KETTLE ON

Singing game

Ritchie family version

Jean calls this a "straight song" now, but in the liner notes of *Children's Songs and Games from the Southern Mountains*, she calls it a "school-ground kissing game."

To play the game, one child stands in the center as the rest of the children join hands to form a ring and march around the circle. At the end of the first stanza, the child in the center chooses a partner; the two swing with a two-hand swing while the others stop marching and clap. The two in the center kiss (or pretend to), and the chosen partner remains in the center as the new "it," while the first child joins the circle.

In *A Garland of Mountain Song*, Jean writes: "Mom Ritchie told me, 'In the old days dancing to the fiddle was thought sinful for us boys and girls; but these kissing games—why, even the preacher thought they were civil and there was no harm in them so long as older folks were there.'"

Viper High School freshman class, circa 1936–37. Jean is in the second row, fourth from the left.

KING WILLIAM

Singing game
Abigail Ritchie version

Jean, all dressed up for a dance, probably at Viper, around 1937 or 1938.

Jean learned this tune from her mother, who remembered it from her own childhood. In our 2007 interview, Jean recalled that the singing game had "verses about 'on the carpet you must kneel' and 'choose the one you love the best,' and so on like that." According to Jean, her mother remembered only the first verse and its striking tune.

In *The American Play-Party Song*, B. A. Botkin cites a source who claims that the game was played in Kentucky "when Daniel Boone was a boy." (Boone was born in 1734.) And Iona Opie notes in *The Singing Game* that "King William" was unusual in the fact that it was better known and earlier recorded in the U.S. than in the U.K. Many variations on the text exist; this one from Workington, England, recorded in 1960, echoes the version Jean learned from her mother:

> King William was King David's son,
> All the royal race is run.
> Choose from the east and choose from the west,
> Choose the one that you love best.
> Down on this carpet you shall kneel,
> While the grass grows 'round your heel.
> Salute your bride and kiss her sweet,
> Rise again upon your feet.

LONDON'S BRIDGE

Singing game
Jason Ritchie version

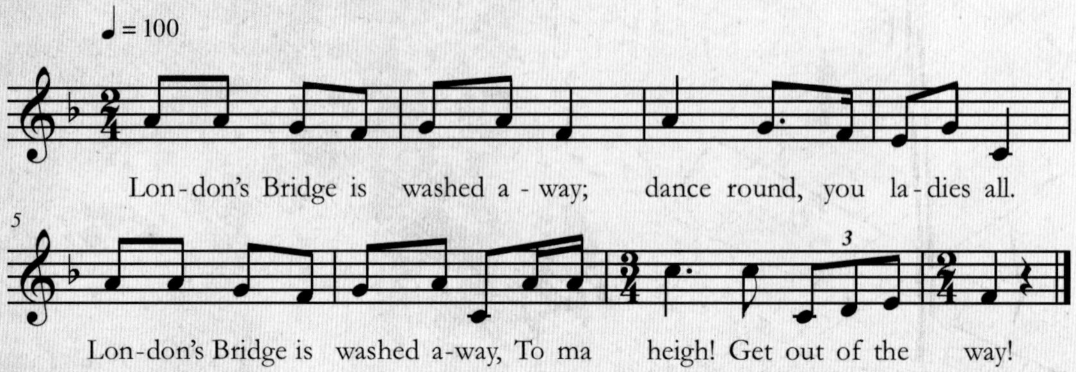

Jean's niece Joy Ritchie poses on a creek bridge near Viper. Jean's handwritten caption on the back reads, "Niece Joy Ritchie, wearing Grandmother (her great-grandmother) Katty Ritchie's bonnet, looking much like Jean did as a little girl. Walk-log behind our house in Viper."

Jean's "Uncle Jason" was one of the "song hunters" of the family. A lawyer by trade, Jason Ritchie was actually a first cousin of Jean's father. This version of "London Bridge" is his.

According to Jean, the Kentucky landscape lends new meaning to this song.

> *In the mountains of Kentucky, you thought of everything being "washed away." When the rains came, the little narrow valleys . . . the streams in the bottom would rise very quickly, and they'd wash away the bridges. The swinging bridges were built very high above the river, but sometimes the river got high enough to wash 'em down. So that's why it's worded that way, I think:*

London's Bridge is washed away;
Dance round, you ladies all.
London's Bridge is washed away,
To ma heigh! Get out of the way!

> *They're marching through the arch; all the children are . . . it's the regular London Bridge game. And when you say "heigh," you catch somebody; the arms come down and you catch somebody. And then they sing the other verses:*

How do we build it up again;
Dance round, you ladies all.
How do we build it up again,
To ma heigh! Get out of the way!

> *And then they sing it: "What's the prisoner done to you?" "Stole my watch and broke my chain," and "Off to prison he must go." That's all sung. It's that nice, pretty tune that Uncle Jason had.*

Uncle Jason Ritchie.

MOMMY, MOMMY, I AM SICK

Jump rope rhyme

Abigail Ritchie version

Recounting this rhyme, Jean said, "This is a rope-jumping rhyme, and it has another chant-like tune."

> Mommy, Mommy, I am sick.
> Call the doctor, quick, quick, quick.
> Doctor, doctor, will I die?
> Yes, my child, but don't you cry.
> How many roses will I have?
> One, two, three, four . . .
> (quickly) . . . seven, eight, nine, ten . . .
> (slowly) eleven, twelve . . .

"You give 'em a hot pepper and cold pepper, until they miss."

I asked, "And you mix it up?"

Jean explained, "Yes, you mix it up and don't tell 'em when it's going to happen. So when the jumper, who's jumping the rope, misses, well . . . the contest is, each one has a turn, and they try to jump the highest number before they miss."

Off to New York City! Jean in 1947.

OLD ROGER IS DEAD

Singing game
Ritchie family version

2. They planted an apple tree over his head,
   Over his head, over his head.
   They planted an apple tree over his head,
   High-o, over his head.

3. The apples got ripe and they all tumbled down, etc.
4. There came an old woman a-picking them up, etc.
5. Old Roger got up and give her a thump, etc.
6. Which made the old woman go hippity-hop, etc.

"Old Roger" is a "drama song," according to Jean, and she learned it at school. "We used to love to play it," she recalled. She included it in her 1964 *The Swapping Song Book*, illustrated with photos of Jean's niece Judy Ritchie (later Hudson) and Jack Hoskins. The photos were taken by Jean's husband, award-winning photographer George Pickow. Jean explained the game as she played it as a girl:

> *"Old Roger Is Dead" is a game, usually played by children walking in a circle around the person playing the part of Old Roger, who lies "dead" on the ground. Another player acts the part of the apple tree, and a third one is the old woman who creeps in and steals the apples. Old Roger springs to life and chases her around. You might want to play it that way.*

The ritual-type game stems from an ancient custom of planting a tree or flower on the grave of one's beloved and the belief that the soul of the deceased went into the plant. It first appeared in print in both England and the United States around the mid-1800s, and while "Old Roger" is most frequently the name of the departed, he is also known in some versions as "Poor Rodger," "Poor Tommy" (in Edinburgh), "Poor Johnnie" (in Suffolk), "Poor Toby" (in Belfast), and even "Poor Gracie" (in Aberdeen). "Cock Robin" and "Oliver Cromwell" sometimes stand in for "Old Roger" as well.

Jean's niece Judy Ritchie and Jack Hoskins play "Old Roger Is Dead."

POOR LITTLE KITTY PUSS

George Pickow based this oil painting on his 1950 photo of the same scene in Kentucky. In the custom shown here, a cat was gently tossed onto a quilt held by four single young women; traditionally, the one nearest where the cat scampered down would be the next to marry.

Jean described this as "a sad little poem; it's a song, really." Jean and I got "tickled" singing the "Kentucky" rhyming scheme in this short ditty during my visit to her Port Washington home. ("And we know what they mean by 'meller.'" As Jean said, laughing, it means "mellow.")

Sometimes children play a game in which they try to sing the song while keeping an appropriately straight face, while one "it" goes around the group, pretending to dry their tears. The first one to giggle is out!

Jack Hoskins, Judy Ritchie, and a friend at play.

THE OLD SOAP GOURD

Singing game
Abigail Ritchie version

Abigail Ritchie knew this play-party game from her own childhood, and Jean learned it from her. Photographer George Pickow (Jean's husband) captured a delightful image of Abigail for *The Swapping Song Book*; in it, she shows gourds of various shapes and sizes to her curious grandchildren. In the book, Jean writes: "When Grandmother was little, they made their own soap in huge black iron kettles, and when it was finished, it was so soft you could just dip up in your hand as much as you needed at a time, and this soft soap was stored in that big gourd in the kitchen." As she explains, "the boys are called 'soap-gourds' for fun, and the girls are 'lily-bushes.'"

The game begins with children forming a ring and walking around one boy in the center. The center boy is blindfolded, and he turns around until, at the end of the second stanza, he stops, and the girl nearest to where he is pointing joins him in the center. The two players in the center then swing each other while the children forming the circle stand still and clap their hands. The boy in the center then leaves the girl and becomes part of the ring, and the game continues with the "lily-bush" (girl) in the center.

Jean's mother, Abigail Hall Ritchie, shows the Ritchie cousins a homemade salt gourd. The gourd on the wall was used for drinking, while the large gourd on the porch was used for soap.

TWO DUKES A-ROVIN'

Singing game

Abigail Ritchie version

2. What is your good will, sir,
   Good will, sir, good will, sir?
   What is your good will, sir?
   To my high-o ransom tee.

3. Our will it is to marry,
   To marry, to marry.
   Our will it is to marry,
   To my high-o ransom tee.

4. You look too brown and drowsy,
   And drowsy, and drowsy.
   You look too brown and drowsy,
   To my high-o ransom tee.

5. We're quite as fair as you are,
   As you are, as you are.
   We're quite as fair as you are,
   To my high-o ransom tee.

6. Who'd you like to marry,
   To marry, to marry?
   Who'd you like to marry?
   To my high-o ransom tee.

7. I'd like to marry Jenny,
   Oh Jenny, oh Jenny.
   I'd like to marry Jenny,
   To my high-o ransom tee.

This singing game is played all over the world, with the "two dukes" marching toward a line of children and then retreating as the children march forward to sing their verses. Sometimes the game ends with the chosen child joining the dukes, and the game continues with "three dukes."

Jean learned this tune from her mother. In our interview, she recalled playing it as a tug-of-war, saying, "Maybe Jenny is stronger than he is, or not. . . . If she pulls him over, he has to go to *her* side."

She sings a slightly different version (with guitar accompaniment) on her 1957 album *Children's Songs and Games from the Southern Mountains.* In that game, the dukes ask, "Will you come?" If the answer is "No!" the dukes sing, "Old dirty rag, she won't come out, rinktum-a dinktum a Johnny-o." If she says "Yes!" they respond, "Pretty little girl, she will come out, rinktum-a dinktum a Johnny-o."

Little Leatherwood School, up the raod from Viper, in Perry County. Jean is in the top row, fourth from the left. The original caption reads: Jean Ritchie, teacher, circa 1942–43.

WHO KILLED COCK ROBIN?

Jean Ritchie version

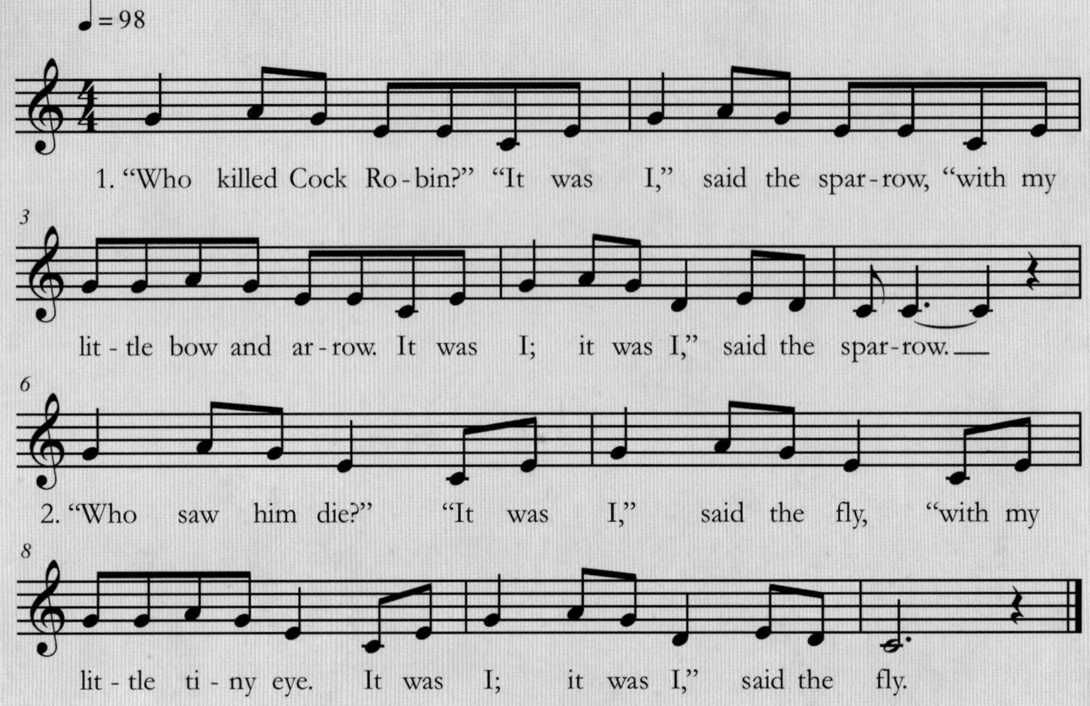

3. "Who caught his blood?"
"It was I," said the fish, "with my little silver dish.
It was I; it was I," said the fish.

4. "Who made his shroud?"
"It was I," said the beetle, "with my little sewing needle.
It was I; it was I," said the beetle.

5. "Who made his coffin?"
"It was I," said the snail, "with my little hammer and nail.
It was I; it was I," said the snail.

6. "Who dug his grave?"
"It was I," said the crow, "with my little spade and hoe.
It was I; it was I," said the crow.

7. "Who lowered him down?"
"It was I," said the crane, "with my little golden chain.
It was I; it was I," said the crane.

8. "Who tolled the bell?"
   "It was I," said the bull; "I's strong and I could pull.
   It was I; it was I," said the bull.

"Who Killed Cock Robin" made its first print appearance in 1744, in *Tommy Thumb's Pretty Song Book*. Jean calls her version a "schoolyard song." She said, "All the children sang it. I guess it came from most of our homes." She recorded two verses for me, and she explained that "it goes through a lot of different animals doing different things, to make the shroud and lower the coffin down, and so on. It's a nice little song."

Jean's full version of the song, accompanied by her dulcimer playing, was recorded for her 1957 *Children's Songs and Games from the Southern Mountains.*

Jean shows her new Jethro Amburgey dulcimer to Lucinda Oakley Ogle, at the Gatlinburg (Tennessee) Handcrafter's Fair in 1947. Mrs. Ogle was a well-known local storyteller, author, and preserver of her family's Smoky Mountain heritage.

M. Sendak

FOUR

Just for Fun: "Straight Songs"

BANDYROWE (KITTY ALONE)

Jean Ritchie version

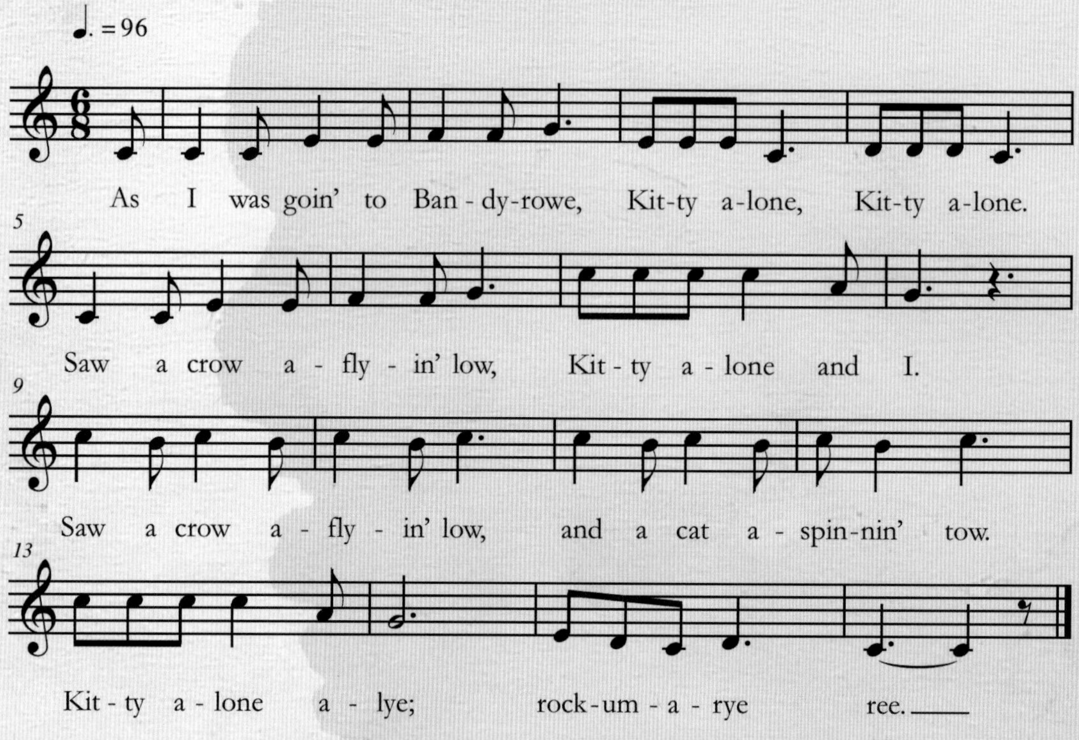

2. In came a little bee, Kitty alone, Kitty alone.
   In came a little bee, Kitty alone, a-lye.
   In came a little bee, with his fiddle across his knee.
   Kitty alone a-lye; rock-um-a-rye ree.

3. Next came in was two small ants, Kitty alone, Kitty alone.
   Next came in was two small ants, Kitty alone, a-lye.
   Next came in was two small ants, fixin' round to have a dance.
   Kitty alone a-lye; rock-um-a-rye ree.

4. Next came in was little Jon, Kitty alone, Kitty alone.
   Next came in was little Jon, Kitty alone, a-lye.
   Next came in was little Jon, one shoe off and one shoe on.
   Kitty alone a-lye; rock-um-a-rye ree.

5. Next came in was little Pete, Kitty alone, Kitty alone.
   Next came in was little Pete, Kitty alone, a-lye.
   Next came in was little Pete, fixin' round to go to sleep.
   Kitty alone a-lye; rock-um-a-rye ree.

6. As I was goin' to Bandyrowe, Kitty alone, Kitty alone.
   Singin' bye-O baby-O, Kitty alone a-lye.
   As I was goin' to Bandyrowe, singin' bye-O baby-O.
   Kitty alone a-lye; rock-um-a-rye ree.

The "Kitty alone" refrain is also found in "Uncle Rat Went Out to Ride," versions of "The Frog's Courtship" that Jean learned from Seamus Ennis and from Elizabeth Cronin, two iconic singers from Ireland whom Jean met and recorded during her 1951–52 fieldwork there. She recorded this lovely lullaby for the album *Marching Across the Green Grass, and Other American Children's Game Songs*. Jean made up the mythical place Bandyrowe and composed the fourth and fifth verses for her sons, Jon and Peter Pickow.

Jean at Viper High School, circa 1936–37.

BANGUM RID BY THE RIVERSIDE
Aunt Ellen Fields version

Jean, with Aunt Ellen Fields, near Aunt Ellen's barn at Mace's Creek, near Viper, Kentucky.

2. There's a wild boar in these woods,
Dillum down, dillum.
Who'll eat his meat, who'll suck his blood?
Dillum down, dillum.

3. If you would this wild boar see,
Dillum down, dillum.
Blow a blast, he'll come to thee,
Dillum down, dillum.

4. Slapped the horn into his mouth,
Dillum down, dillum.
Blew a blast both north and south,
Dillum down, dillum.

5. Wild boar come in such a rush,
Dillum down, dillum.
Split his way through oak and ash,
Dillum down, dillum.

6. Fit four hours by the day,
Dillum down, dillum.
At last the wild boar run away,
Dillum down, dillum.

7. Old Bangum follered him to his den,
Dillum down, dillum.
Saw the bones of a thousand men,
Dillum down, dillum.

Jean first heard this version of "Old Bangum" from Aunt Ellen Fields, a relative on her mother's side, who learned it from her own father. The tale is a survival of Child ballad no. 18, "Sir Lionel." Jean's own version evolved over the years as she "pieced out the story" with verses from Uncle Jason and her own family's recollections.

BIG GLASS DOLL

Dialogue song
Ritchie family version

3. Sell Pappy's feather bed,
Feather bed, feather bed.
Sell Pappy's feather bed,
Do, Mommy, do.

4. Where shall your Pappy sleep,
Pappy sleep, Pappy sleep?
Where shall your Pappy sleep?
Do, baby, do.

5. Sleep in the horsie's barn,
Horsie's barn, horsie's barn.
Sleep in the horsie's barn,
Do, Mommy, do.

6. Where shall the horsie sleep,
   Horsie sleep, horsie sleep?
   Where shall the horsie sleep?
   Do, baby, do.

7. Tie him to the riverbank,
   The riverbank, the riverbank.
   Tie him to the riverbank,
   Do, Mommy, do.

8. If you don't hush I'll give you a spank,
   Give you a spank, give you a spank.
   If you don't hush I'll give you a spank,
   Do, baby, do.
   (Spank, spank, spank, spank!)

Jean classified this song as one that had long been in the Ritchie family's singing tradition. "I guess I learned it from my older sisters, and they got it from the family. It's been in the family a long time."

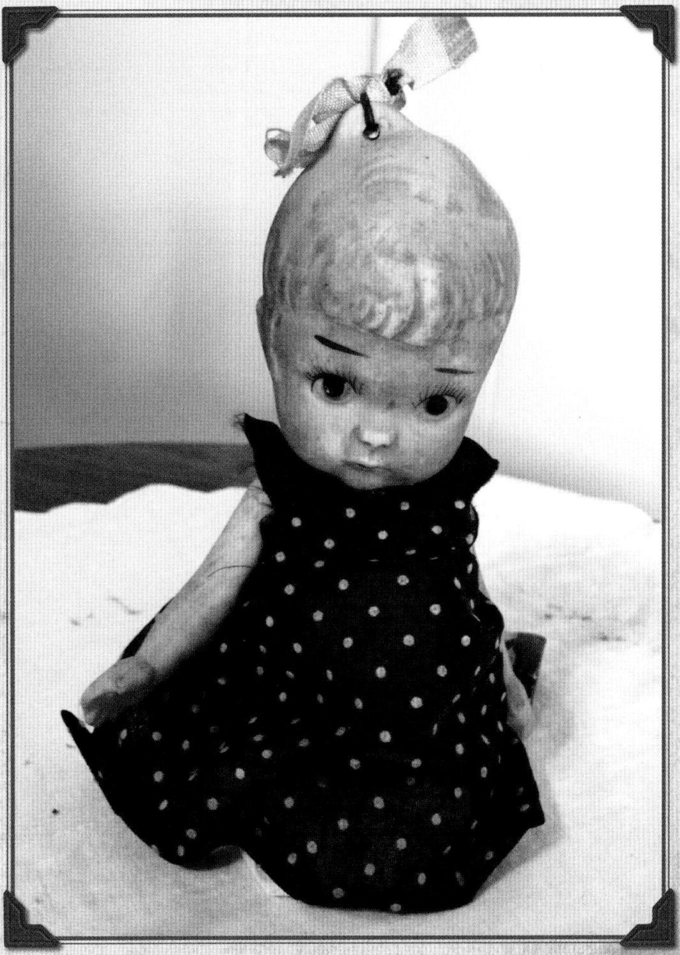

Jean's "glass doll."

BUILT MY LOVE A FINE BRICK HOUSE

Play-party game

Ritchie family version

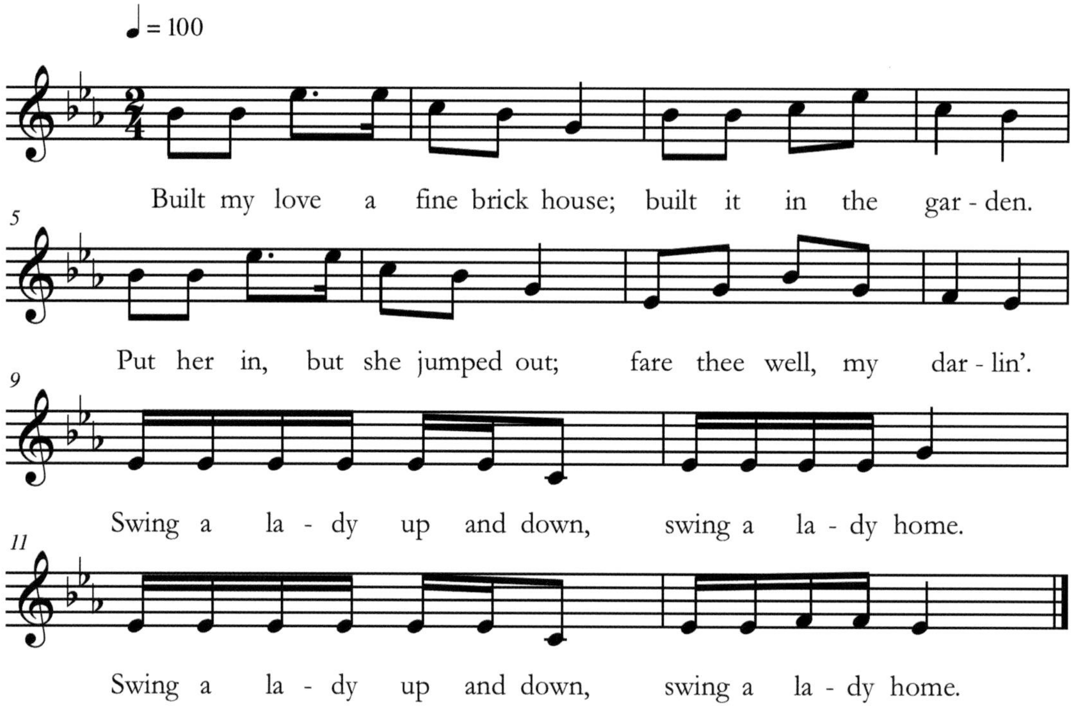

2. Way low down in the cedar swamp,
   Water's deep and muddy.
   It's there I met my pretty little miss;
   There I met my honey.
   Swing a lady up and down . . .

3. Black-eyed girl is mad at me,
   Blue-eyed girl won't have me.
   If I can't have the one I love,
   I guess I'll never marry.
   Swing a lady up and down . . .

4. The older she gets, the prettier she gets,
   I tell you, she's a honey.
   Makes me work all through the week,
   And get stove wood on Sunday!
   Swing a lady up and down . . .

"Built My Love a Fine Brick House" is a play-party song, the kind that Jean remembers boys and girls playing together at the semiannual pie suppers at her school. She provides a vivid description of those social events in her 1965 *Folk Songs of the Southern Appalachians*, in which the song is called "Cedar Swamp." She writes:

> *I remember that the most agonizing time was the hour after we girls had placed our brightly-wrapped and beribboned pies on the auctioneer's table (the two teachers' desks pushed together). Each girl had been given the number of her own pie, with instructions to keep it a secret from the boys, and had been told to "wait in the schoolyard until the bell rings." The moonlight was a witchery; the shadows were alive with the happy shrieks of young children not quite able to bear the heady freedom of the soft wild night. The only thing that kept the whole lot of us from bursting with sheer excitement and joy was our joining together in games, usually singing games, so that we could shout to the top of our lungs, jump and skip, dance pretty in hopes he would notice us, and somehow manage, just barely, to wait for that bell.*

Jack Hoskins builds a "big fine house" as Judy Ritchie watches.

DANCE TO YOUR DADDY

Corn shuck dolls from Jean Ritchie's personal collection, made by Jean's sister May Ritchie Deschamps.

Jean's eldest son added his own contribution to this song when he was young. She explained, "That's our family tune, and Peter, I think, wrote a second verse to it when he was a baby. He didn't write it; he sang it. He thought mammies were being left out. He sang:

"Dance to your mammy, my little lambie,
Dance to your mammy, my little lamb.
You shall have a suppie, in your little cuppie,
You shall have a suppie when the cow comes home."

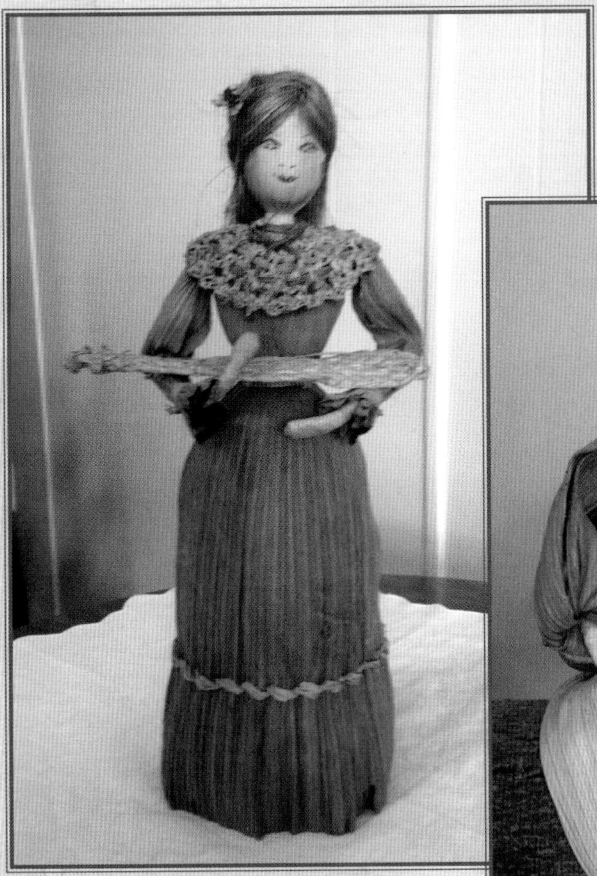

JEMMY TAYLOR-O

2. Jemmy Taylor-O goes downtown.
   All the pretty girls, they follow him around.
   Heigh, ho, diddle-i-dey.

3. Jemmy Taylor-O goin' down the road,
   Singin' like a bullfrog, hoppin' like a toad.
   Heigh, ho, diddle-i-dey.

4. Well, we had a little trouble down the other end of town.
   Nobody hurt, but a feller knocked down.
   Heigh, ho, diddle-i-dey.

5. Come to the place where the blood was shed;
   The boys go back, and the girls go ahead.
   Heigh, ho, diddle-i-dey.

6. The boys and the girls when they do meet,
   They stop and they hug and they kiss about a week.
   Heigh, ho, diddle-i-dey.

7. Poor, poor Jemmy Taylor-O.
   Ain't it a shame about Jemmy Taylor-O?
   Heigh, ho, diddle-i-dey.

Alan Lomax recorded Jean singing "Jimmy Taylor-O" in 1949, during one of their early sessions in New York. The song also appears on several commercial recordings, including the 1954 Elektra LPs *Jean Ritchie* and *Kentucky Mountain Songs*, and the 1979 Greenhays album *High Hills and Mountains.*

The Special Collections & Archives sound archives at Berea College hold a number of video and sound recordings of Jean's live performances there throughout the years. During a 1979 concert at Berea's Celebration of Traditional Music, Jean talked about the history of the song, and learning it as a child:

> *This one is a funny old song; it's not one that anybody ever plays as a game, but it used to be a game. It's called "Jemmy Taylor-O," and we think that it refers to General Zachary Taylor, who was our twelfth President of the United States. He was a Major General when the war with Mexico took place, and we think that "Jemmy Taylor-O" may be just a corruption of "Gen'ral Taylor-O." That's the closest we can come to guessing about it, anyway.*
>
> *You can sort of tell what the action is by listening to the words. It sounds like one of those play-party games where the boy and the girl separate and they meet on the outside. When they meet, they give each other a kiss; it's a kind of a kissing game. Pretty little tune, though, and I just heard it played on banjos and fiddles when I was a little girl.*

Jack Hoskins, Judy Ritchie, and Joy Ritchie on an old-fashioned rail fence.

KILLY KRANKY

Play-party game
Jason Ritchie version

2. Killy Kranky is my song,
Sing and dance it all day long.
From my elbow to my knee,
Now we'll wind the grapevine tree.
Chorus: Broke my arm, broke my arm . . .

3. Killy Kranky is my song,
Sing and dance it all day long.
From my wrist down to my toe,
How much further can you go?
Chorus: Broke my arm, broke my arm . . .

In the liner notes for *Jean Ritchie at Home*, Jean writes,

> *One time when Dad's cousin Jason Ritchie was visiting, he and Dad recollected and sang this bit of a song for me. They remembered that when they were small, all the children in the schoolyard would play this during recess and dinnertimes. They would join hands in a long line, and the leader would reach up his right hand and hold onto one of the schoolhouse logs, his arm making a sort of arch, and they'd start the song. The child on the end of the line would lead the line under this arch so that the one next to the leader would soon be marching in place beside or slightly behind the leader. Everyone had gone under that arch except the leader himself, he stood firm, and his left hand, held by this next-in-line, pulled his left arm around his own neck. The end child then led the line under each arch in turn, and one by one, the left arm of each child was passed in front of his chin and his left hand grasping the next in line was over his right shoulder. The last in line, with nobody holding his left hand, had to pass his own left hand over his right shoulder, turn his body around with this motion, and give his left hand to the leader, who took the hand and completed the close circle, or chain. Once "wound," the leader would call out "fast" or "slow." Eventually the human chain would break up amidst much confusion and laughter.*

Jean thought the words to the song were just nonsense, until a 1951 trip to Scotland. She and husband George were driving through Perthshire and spied a road sign for the tiny village of Killiekrankie. She said, "There actually is such a place! I felt that a very big chain had been completed!"

Jean and George's road sign at Killiekrankie, re-discovered by Susan Brumfield during a 1999 research trip to Scotland.

MAMA TOLD ME (OLD SHOE BOOTS)

Jean plays a tune on her Amburgey dulcimer at the 1947 Handcrafter's Fair in Gatlinburg, Tennessee, as Lucinda Oakley Ogle looks on. Mrs. Ogle worked as a hostess at the posh Mountain View Hotel, seen in the background.

2. Mama told me to bring him a chair;
Oh, I can't, I won't have him.
I brought him a chair and Lord! How he did stare!
With his old shoe boots and his leggin's.

3. Mama told me to bring him a plate;
Oh, I can't, I won't have him.
I brought him a plate and he kicked it in the grate,
With his old shoe boots and his leggin's.

4. Mama told me to bring him a fork;
Oh, I can't, I won't have him.
I brought him a fork, and he told me to go to New York,
With his old shoe boots and his leggin's.

5. Mama told me to bring him a knife;
Oh, I can't, I won't have him.
I brought him a knife and he asked me to be his wife,
With his old shoe boots and his leggin's.

6. Mama told me to fix him some meat;
Oh, I can't, I won't have him.
I fixed him some meat, and Lord! How he did eat,
With his old shoe boots and his leggin's.

7. Mama told me to make up his bed;
Oh, I can't, I won't have him.
I made up his bed, and I wish't that he was dead,
With his old shoe boots and his leggin's.

8. Mama told me to cover him well;
Oh, I can't, I won't have him.
I covered him well, and he snored like the devil,
With his old shoe boots and his leggin's.

Folklorist Kenneth Goldstein wrote the liner notes for Jean's 1957 recording *Children's Songs and Games from the Southern Mountains*. He notes two different versions of this song from Scotland, which he dates as "over two hundred years old." In addition to the "old shoe boots and leggin's" of the Ritchie family version, there is an "old grey beard newly shaven" version, too.

In our interview, Jean called this "lament song," mourning the disadvantages of being a young girl courted by an old man, "downright funny." She recalled that her older sister Una used to sing "Mama Told Me" to the "young 'uns," and it is still thought of in the family as a children's song.

MAMMY HAD AN OLD GOOSE

3. Well, the gun it wouldn't shoot her, homey halley ho.
The gun it wouldn't shoot her, homey halley ho.
Chorus: 'Cause weren't she an old goose . . .

4. Well, they throwed her in the hog pen, homey halley ho.
They throwed her in the hog pen, homey halley ho.

5. And she broke the old sow's teeth out, homey halley ho.
She broke the old sow's teeth out, homey halley ho.
Chorus: Weren't she an old goose . . .

6. Well, they put her on the table, homey halley ho.
They put her on the table, homey halley ho.

7. Well, the fork, it wouldn't gouge her, homey halley ho.
And the knife it wouldn't cut her, homey halley ho.
Chorus: Weren't she an old goose . . .

Jean learned this song from John and Ben Hall at the John C. Campbell Folk School in Brasstown, North Carolina. She recorded it for *Children's Songs and Games from the Southern Mountains*. It is a variant of the African-American song "The Grey Goose."

Jack Hoskins, Judy Ritchie, and Joy Ritchie "walking the rails."

MY GOOD OLD MAN

Ha'nt song
Ritchie family version

Spoken: "Goin' to town."

2. What are you goin' to buy there, my good old man? ("Buy me a gun.")
3. What you want a gun for, my good old man? ("Keep the bears away from you.")
4. What d'ya want for your supper, my good old man? ("Bushel eggs.")
5. Bushel eggs'll kill you, my good old man. ("Don't care if they do.")
6. Where d'ya want to be buried at, my good old man? ("In the chimney corner.")
7. Ashes'll fall on you, my good old man. ("Don't care if they do.")
8. What d'ya want to be buried there for, my good old man? ("So I can scare the devil out of your next old man!")

Jean wrote about the "ha'nt songs" she listened to as a child in *Singing Family of the Cumberlands*. When Granny Katty came for a visit, everyone knew that there would be talk among the older folks about the ghosts and ha'nts they'd seen in their time. After an evening of scary songs and tales around the fire, the young ones would be sent off to bed. Too "scaredy" to sleep, they'd try to spook each other with ghost noises, tapping and tickling. "After 'Skin and Bones,'" Jean says, "'My Good Old Man' was still ha'nty enough to belong with the ghosty feeling we all had, but not too fearsome to make a child cry."

Judy Ritchie with a musically inclined scarecrow.

OLD DADDY GRUMBLE

Dialogue song
Ritchie family version

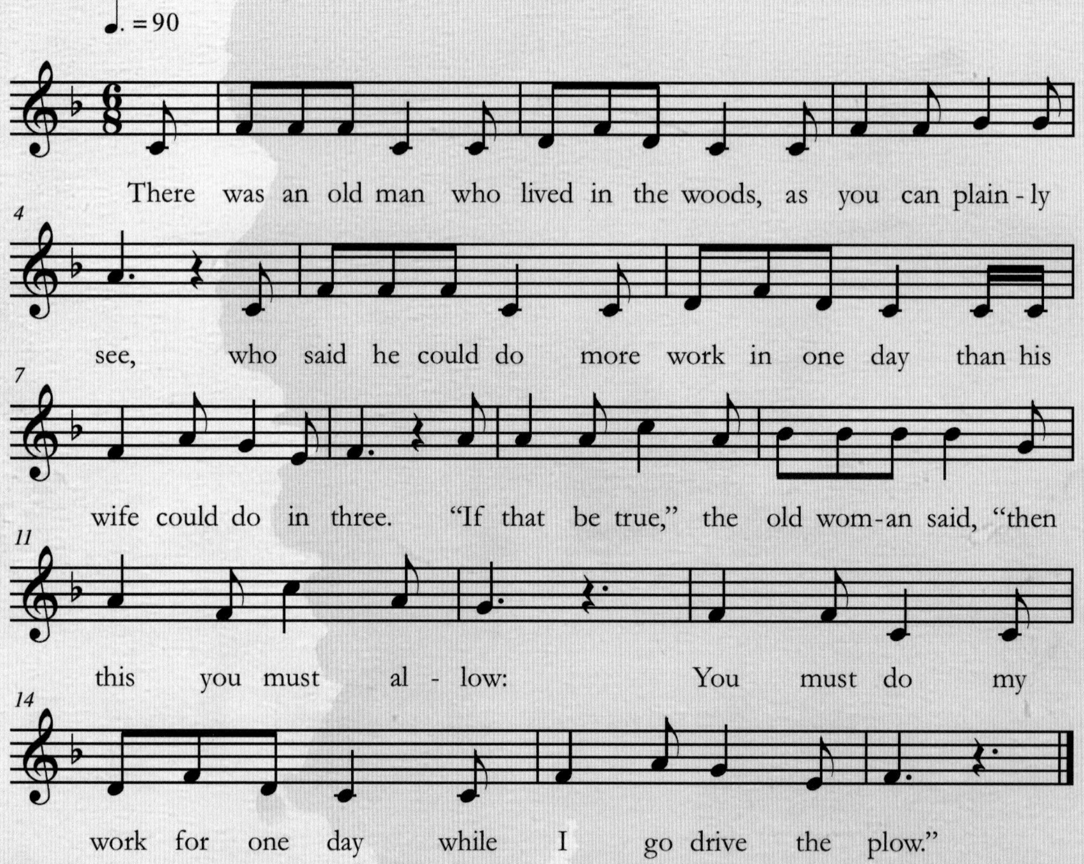

2. "Now you must milk the Tiny cow, for fear she should go dry,
And you must feed the little pigs that are within the sty.
And you must watch the speckled hen, lest she should lay astray,
And you must wind the reel of yarn that I spun yesterday."

3. The old woman took the staff in her hand and went to drive the plow.
The old man took the pail in his hand and went to milk the cow.
But Tiny hitched, and Tiny switched, and Tiny cocked her nose,
And Tiny gave the old man such a kick that the blood ran down to his toes.

4. (spoken) "Now it's HEY my good cow, and HO my good cow, and NOW my good cow, stand still!
(sung) If I ever milk this cow again, it'll be against my will."
But Tiny hitched, and Tiny switched, and Tiny cocked her nose,
And Tiny gave the old man such a kick that the blood ran down to his toes.

5. Well, when he had milked the Tiny cow, for fear she should go dry,
Why, then he fed the little pigs that are within the sty.
And then he watched the speckled hen, lest she should lay astray,
But he forgot the reel of yarn his wife spun yesterday.

6. He swore by all the stars in the sky, and all the leaves on the tree,
That his wife could do more work in one day than he could do in three.
He swore by all the leaves on the tree and all the stars in heaven,
That his wife could do more work in one day than he could do in seven!

This song is also known as "Old Father Grumble" and "The Old Man in the Woods." Jean learned this version from one of her sisters, who brought it from the Pine Mountain Settlement School. She included it in *The Swapping Song Book*, illustrated with photos of her parents milking a cow: "Grandmother Abigail couldn't keep a straight face and she laughed right out loud. She said, 'Put you a dress on if you're so set on milking her, for that's the only way you'll ever fool this cow.'"

Jean's father, Balis Ritchie, milks a stubborn cow, as wife Abigail looks on.

OLD KING COLE WAS A JOLLY OLD SOUL

Gettin'-up game
Ritchie family version

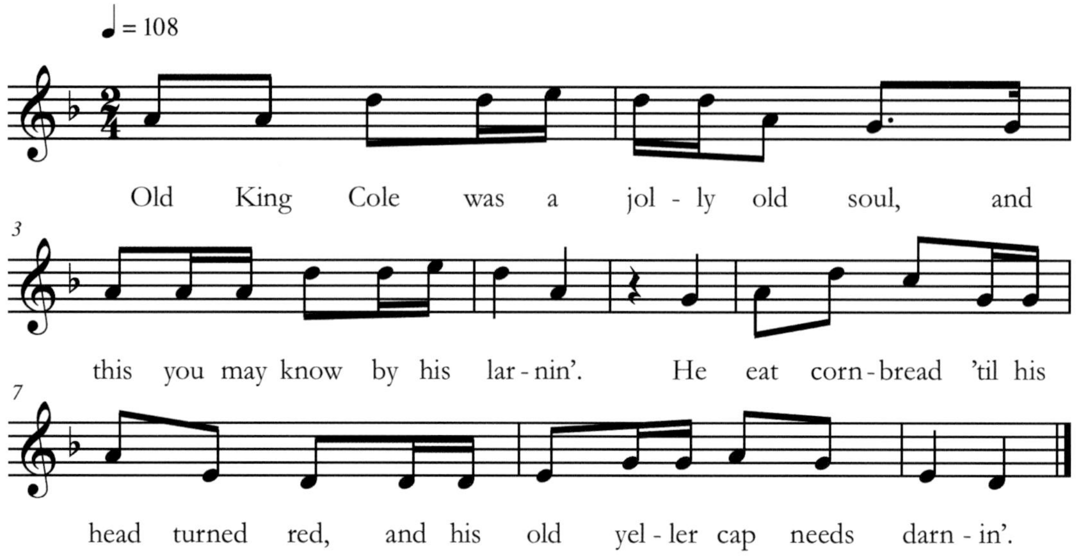

2. My pretty little pink, I once did think that you and I would marry,
But now I've lost all hopes of you, and I ain't got long to tarry.

3. Where the coffee grows on the white oak tree, and the rivers, they run brandy,
Where the boys are as pure as a lump of gold and the girls are sweet as candy.

4. I'll take my knapsack on my back, my musket on my shoulder.
I'll march away to Mexico; enlist and be a soldier.

5. You may go on and I'll turn back to the place where we first parted.
We'll open up the ring and choose a couple in, and we hope they'll come free-hearted.

Jean said that her father called this song, popular at play-parties, "a gettin'-up game." He and Jean's mother and the other courting couples would use it to start the evening's party off, when everyone was too bashful to take partners. "At last," she recalled, "one brave couple would promenade round the room singing this song, and when they got to the line, 'We'll open up the ring and choose a couple in,' another boy would have got up nerve to ask a girl up, and they'd come in. Then the four of them would begin the game song all over again, and keep it up until they had enough players on the floor for 'Boston' or 'Charlie.'"

Jean discovered the roots of the tune in Ireland, during her 1951–52 field trip. She visited Sarah Makem in her home and recorded Mrs. Makem singing "As I Roved Out" (all while Mrs. Makem was baking bread and putting bacon in the pan). Its text is completely different, but the tune is nearly identical to the Ritchie family's tune for "Old King Cole."

Jean's song and dance group from Viper High School performs at the County Fair at Quicksand, circa 1937.

OLD KING QUINE

Jason Ritchie version

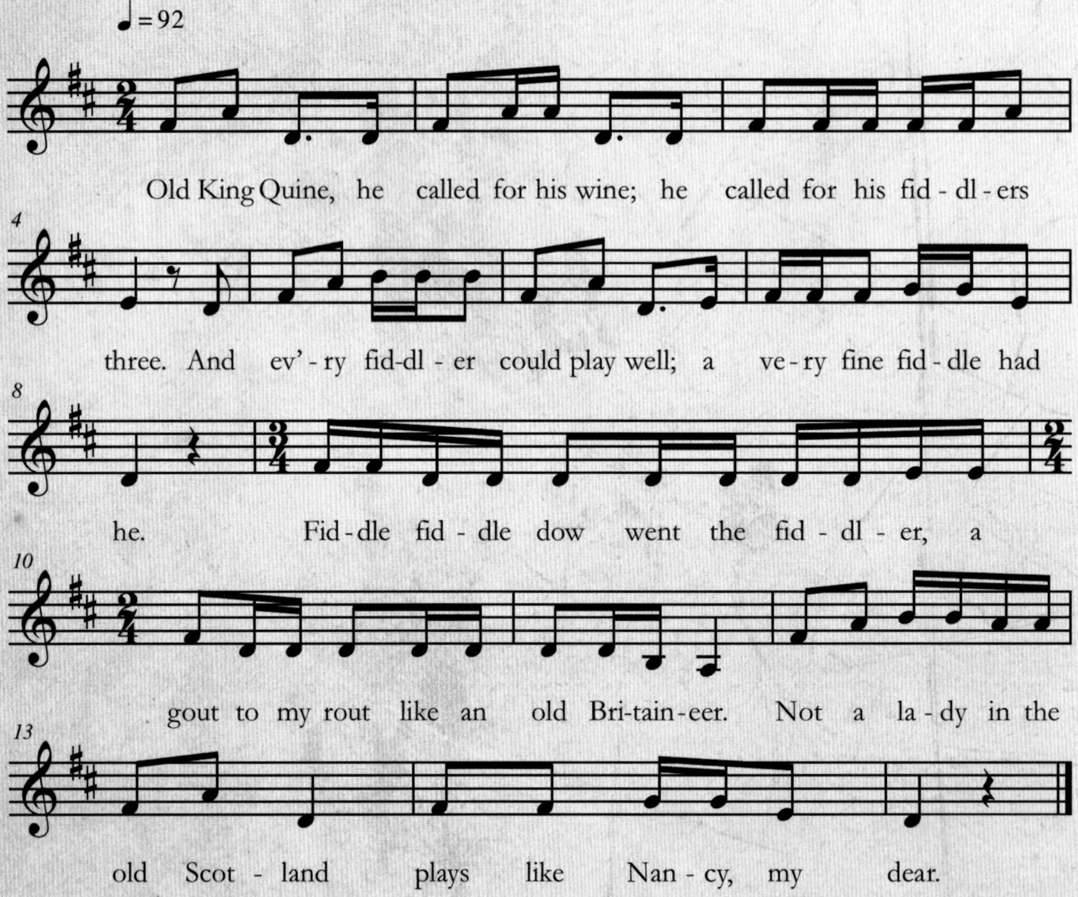

Jean recalled this version of "Old King Quine" as another one of Uncle Jason's tunes. The words are related to those of "Old King Cole." (The Ritchie family version of "Old King Cole," sung at play-parties as another "gettin'-up game," contains only the first line of that well-known rhyme.) The last line is directly related to a 1776 version from the Herd manuscript, *Scots Songs and Ballads*, which ends with the line "There's no' a lass in all Scotland, compared to our sweet Margarie."

Jean recorded this song with a slightly different tune and text on *Marching Across the Green Grass, and Other American Children's Game Songs*:

> Old King Quine, he sent for his wine; he sent for his fiddlers three.
> Every fiddler fiddled so well, under the greenwood tree.
> Saw-saw-saw went the fiddlers-O, Saw-saw-saw went the fiddlers-O!
> We'll all feel fine if we take a little wine, and fiddle with old King Quine.

In the liner notes, Jean explains:

> *On the schoolyard at morning recess, my friends and I liked to improvise instruments (for instance, two sticks became a fiddle) and act out this song in our own way. We went to a two-room school—primer through third grades in one room with the "little-room" teacher, and the fourth through eighth grades in the other room with the principal. Our schoolhouse was a small, white frame building with a bell tower in front, and it was bounded on one side by the river and a long mountain ridge, and on the other side by the county road, the L&N tracks and another long mountain ridge. Our playground was yellow dirt, hard packed and smooth, and around the edges were grass and daisies and trees. . . . So we really were "under the greenwood tree" when we play-acted "Old King Quine."*

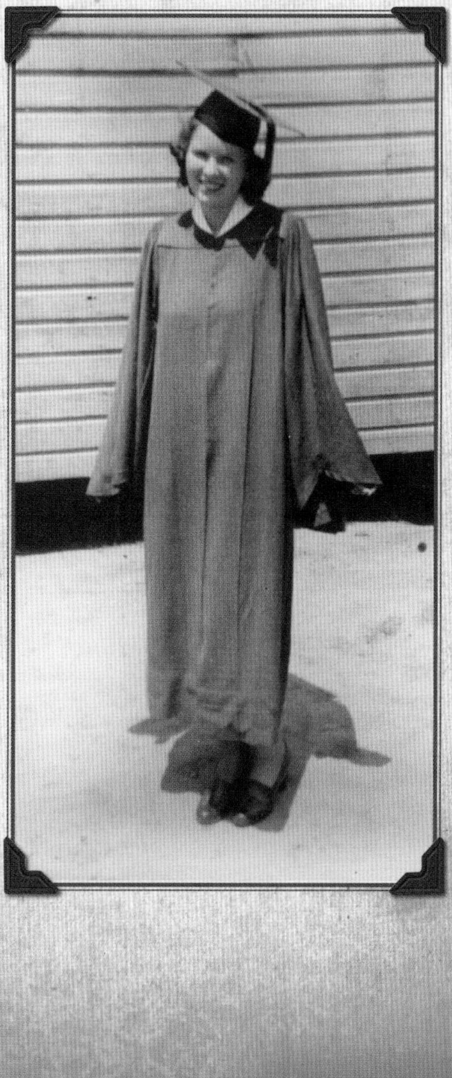

Graduation Day! Viper High School, circa 1938–39.

SKIN AND BONES

Ha'nt song

Ritchie family version

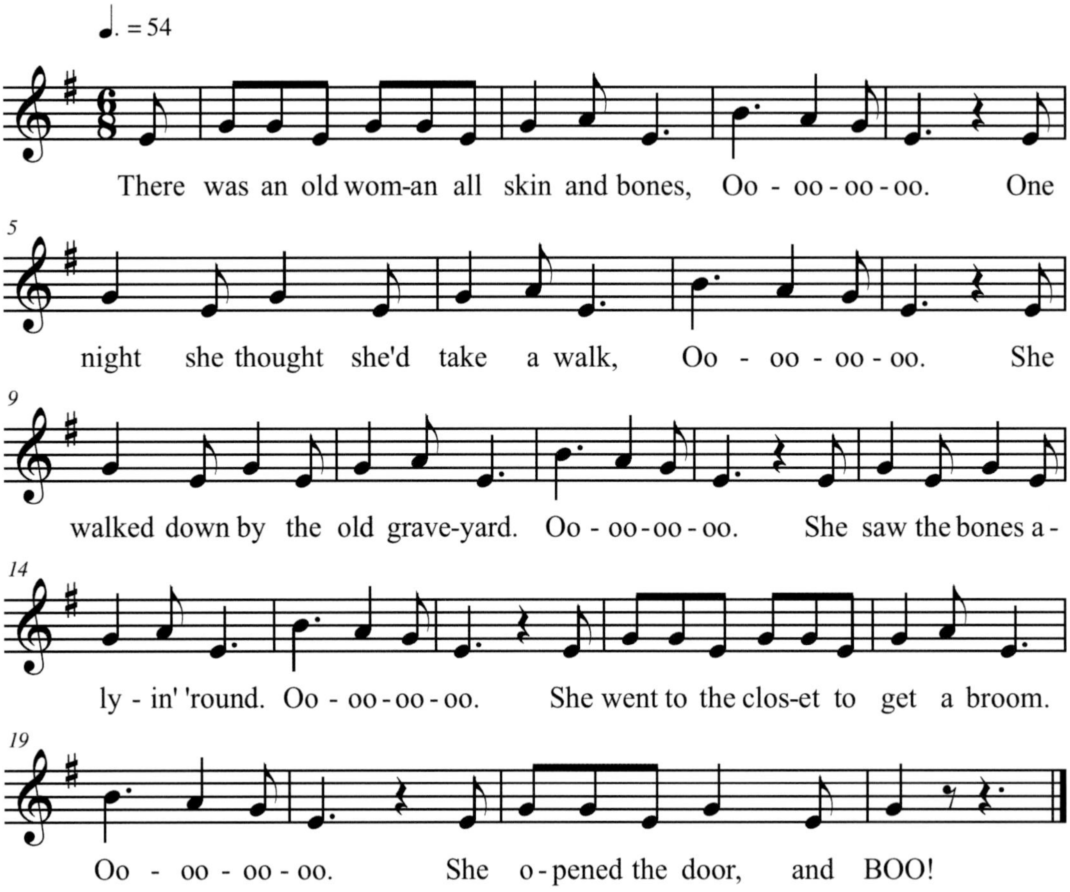

The Ritchie family version of "Skin and Bones" is unique, with its "bones a-lyin' 'round" and closet and broom plot device. It is surely related to the scary tales of "The Old Woman in the Churchyard" or "The Old Woman of Skin and Bone" popular throughout England, Scotland, and Ireland. The details are slightly different, but the telling of the tale is always the same: eerily quiet and spooky, ending with a big "BOO!" and screams all around.

In *Folk Songs of the Southern Appalachians*, Jean writes, "We liked it best when there was someone in the room who hadn't heard it before; all of us would jump with fright and surprise at the end, no matter how many times we'd sung it before, but that person would jump the highest and holler the loudest. We always loved to sing it, even if just the family was there whenever we told ha'nt tales around the fireplace on winter evenings."

Jack Hoskins and Judy Ritchie in the Hall family graveyard, Viper, Kentucky.

SOLDIER, SOLDIER

Dialogue song
Balis Ritchie version

"Oh, solder, soldier, will you marry me,
With your musket, fife and drum?"
"Oh no, pretty lady, I cannot marry you,
For I have no shirt to put on."
Then away she ran to the shirt-maker's shop,
As fast as she could run.
And she bought him a shirt of the very best kind,
And the soldier put it on.

This tune variation of the well-known "acting out" song comes from Jean's father. She explained, "It goes on and on, down to the shoes. And finally, he says he's got a wife at home, and so on . . . no tellin' what she's gonna do to him then!"

> "Oh, no, pretty lady, I cannot marry you,
> For I have a wife at home!"

Jean sings "Lazy John," an old North Carolina variant of the song, on her 1968 recording *Marching Across the Green Grass, and Other American Children's Game Songs*.

Jean's handwritten caption on the back of this photo reads, "Balis Ritchie watering Helen, the cow."

THE HUNTING TALE

Jason Ritchie version

2. I tracked a sally buck all day; I tracked him through the snow.
   I tracked him to the water's edge, and under he did go,
   O, and under he did go.

3. I loaded up my pistol, sir, and under then I went.
   To kill the fattest buck, sir, it was my whole intent,
   O, it was my whole intent.

4. I went down in the waters, ten thousand feet or more.
   I fired off my pistol, like a cannon she did roar,
   O, like a cannon she did roar.

5. Out of ten and twenty big fat bucks, by chance I did get one.
   The rest, they raised their bristles up and at me they did run,
   O, and at me they did run.

6. My hide was riddled full of holes; ten bullfrogs, they jumped through.
   I stabbed my sword into the holes, and all those frogs I slew,
   O, and all those frogs I slew.

7. I bent my gun in a circle, and I fired her round the hill.
   Out of ten and twenty big fat bucks, ten thousand did I kill,
   O, ten thousand did I kill.

8. To the moon I sold my venison, to the stars I sold my skins.
The man that tells the biggest lies commits the biggest sins,
O, commits the biggest sins.

In *Singing Family of the Cumberlands*, Jean recalls her first meeting with "Uncle Jason" Ritchie, one of the most prolific song collectors in the family. Jason told her that many of his songs were handed down from Jean's great-great-grandfather Crockett Ritchie or from old singers like Will Wooten, who had probably learned them from Crockett, too. This one came from a play-party. (According to Jason, that was the best place to learn more songs, since that was the place where songs got swapped around the most.) Jean categorized this one as a "straight song" (a song without a game). Uncle Jason said, "When young folks'd get tired, they'd sit around the fireside and sing for hours on end, or sometimes just until they got their wind back for the games. No, there wasn't much singing all together. Just everybody sang what he knew, all round the circle."

Jack Hoskins, Judy Ritchie, and Cindy Gordon explore a river.

THE TREE IN THE VALLEY-O

Cumulative song

Ritchie family version

4. There was a twig and a very fine twig,
And the finest twig you ever did see.
And the twig was on the limb, and the limb was on the branch,
And the branch was on the tree,
And the tree was away down in the valley-o.

5. There was a nest and a very fine nest,
And the finest nest you ever did see.
And the nest was on the twig, and the twig was on the limb,
And the limb was on the branch, and the branch was on the tree,
And the tree was away down in the valley-o.

6. There was an egg, etc.
7. There was a bird, etc.
8. There was a wing, etc.
9. There was a feather, etc.
10. There was a bug, etc.

Judy Ritchie and Jack Hoskins climb a tree.

WHERE ARE YOU GOING, LITTLE BIRDIE?

Dialogue song
Jean Ritchie version

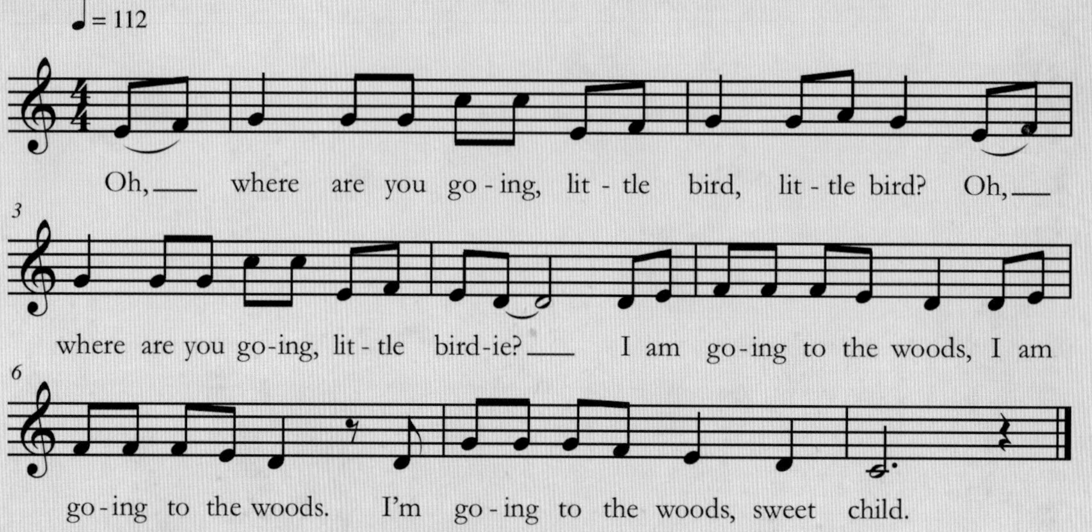

Jean teaching at the Henry Street Settlement School in New York City, circa 1947.

Jean recalled learning this song from one of her school friends:

I learned [this song] on the school-ground from a little girl who didn't live in the community long. She was the daughter of a railroad operator who lived just a short time in that house up at Viper. Her name was Blanche White.

Oh, where are you going, little bird, little bird?
Oh, where are you going, little birdie?
I am going to the woods, I am going to the woods,
I'm going to the woods, sweet child.

Oh, what's in the woods, little bird, little bird?
Oh, what's in the woods, little birdie?
There's a tree in the woods, there's a tree in the woods,
There's a tree in the woods, sweet child.

And that goes on until . . . the last verse is . . . they discover that in the tree there's a nest, and there are eggs, and in the eggs there are some birds, and the birds . . . and you ask:

Oh, what do they say, little bird, little bird?
Oh, what do they say, little birdie?
They can say, "Praise the Lord," they can say, "Praise the Lord."
They can say, "Praise the Lord," sweet child.

Or some say:

They can say, "peep, peep, peep," they can say, "peep, peep, peep."

The ones that don't want to be religious sing that. [Laughing.] And that's the way it ends.

Bibliography

Books and Articles

Brumfield, Susan. *Hot Peas and Barley-O: Children's Songs and Games from Scotland.* Milwaukee, WI: Hal Leonard, 2006.

Green, Percy B. *A History of Nursery Rhymes.* London: Greening and Co., 1899. NOOK edition ed. Amanda Lee, Five Star Publishing, 2013.

Herd, David. *Ancient and Modern Scottish Songs, Heroic Ballads, etc. in Two Volumes* (manuscript). Edinburgh: National Library of Scotland, 1776.

Jones, Loyal. "Jean Ritchie: Twenty-Five Years After." *Appalachian Journal* Vol. 8, No. 3 (Spring 1981): 224–29.

Newell, William Wells. *Games and Songs of American Children.* New York: Dover Publications, 1883, 1903, 1963.

Opie, Peter, and Iona Opie. *The Singing Game.* New York: Oxford University Press, 1985.

Ritchie, Jean. *Apple Seeds and Soda Straws: Love Charms and Legends Written Down for Young and Old.* New York: H.Z. Walck, 1965.

Ritchie, Jean. *Celebration of Life.* Port Washington, NY: Geordie Music Publishing, 1971.

Ritchie, Jean. *The Dulcimer Book.* New York: Oak Publications, 1963.

Ritchie, Jean. *Dulcimer People.* New York: Oak Publications, 1975.

Ritchie, Jean. *Folk Songs of the Southern Appalachians, as Sung by Jean Ritchie.* New York: Oak Publications, 1965; reprint, Lexington: University Press of Kentucky, 1997.

Ritchie, Jean. *From Fair to Fair.* New York: H.Z. Walck, 1966.

Ritchie, Jean. *A Garland of Mountain Song.* New York: Broadcast Music, 1953.

Ritchie, Jean. *Singing Family of the Cumberlands.* New York: Oxford University Press, 1955; reprint, Oak Publications, 1963; reprint, Geordie Music Publishing, 1980; reprint, Lexington: University Press of Kentucky, 1988.

Ritchie, Jean. *The Swapping Song Book*. New York: Oak Publications, 1965; reprint, Lexington: University Press of Kentucky, 1999.

Ritchie, Jean. *Traditional Mountain Dulcimer*. New York: Homespun Tapes, 1984.

Audio Recordings

Childhood Songs. Greenhays, 1991. GR90723 [audio-cassette].

Dear Jean: Artists Celebrate Jean Ritchie. Compass Records, 2014. COM 4631 [2-CD set].

High Hills and Mountains. Greenhays, 1979. GR70708 [CD (with *None But One*)].

Kentucky Mountain Songs. Elektra-Stratford, 1954. EKL-25 [LP].

Jean Ritchie Sings Children's Songs and Games from the Southern Mountains. Smithsonian Folkways, 1957. 07054 [LP].

Jean Ritchie at Home. Pacific Cascade Records, 1975. 7026 [LP].

Marching Across the Green Grass, and Other American Children's Game Songs. Asch Records AH 752, 1968; Smithsonian Folkways, 1992. FC 7702. [LP].

Saturday Night and Sunday Too. Riverside, 1956. RLP 12-620 [LP].

The Most Dulcimer. Greenhays, 1984. GR70714 [CD].

The Ritchie Family of Kentucky. Smithsonian Folkways, 1959. 02316 [LP].

Video Recordings

Mountain Born: The Jean Ritchie Story. Prod. H. Russell Farmer and Guy Mendez. Videotape: Kentucky Educational Television, 1996; DVD: PBS Educational Media, pbs.org, MBJR401.

Permissions/Credits

Song Text and Music Credits

"Bandyrowe," "Bangum Rid by the Riverside," "Dance to Your Daddy," "Darby's Ram," "Mama Told Me," "The Death of Cock Robin" ("Who Killed Cock Robin"), © copyright 1965 Geordie Music Publishing. Used by permission.

"Built My Love a Big Fine House," "Two Dukes a' Roving" © copyright 1940 Jean Ritchie, 1965 Geordie Music Publishing. Used by permission.

"God Bless the Moon," "Jenny, Put Your Kettle On," music and new words by Jean Ritchie © copyright 1969, 1971 Geordie Music Publishing. Used by permission.

"Golden Ring Around the Susan Girl," words and new music by Jean Ritchie © copyright 1963, 1971 Geordie Music Publishing. Used by permission.

"Jemmy Taylor-O," "Old Daddy Grumble," "The Hunting Tale," new and additional words and music Jean Ritchie © copyright 1971 Geordie Music Publishing. Used by permission.

"Killy Kranky," new and additional words and music Jean Ritchie © copyright 1965, 1971 Geordie Music Publishing. Used by permission.

"Old King Cole," © copyright 1953 BMI. Used by permission.

"Among the Little White Daisies," "London's Bridge," © copyright 1965 Geordie Music Publishing. Used by permission.

"Skin and Bones," new and additional words and music Jean Ritchie © copyright 1952 Geordie Music, Inc. Used by permission.

"The Old Soap Gourd," Ritchie family version, words and music Jean Ritchie © copyright 1952 Geordie Music, Inc. Used by permission.

All other songs © copyright Jean Ritchie. Used by permission.

Reprinted in *The Swapping Song Book* © copyright 1999 University of Kentucky Press: "Built My Love a Big Fine House," "Hush Little Baby," "Old Daddy Grumble," "Old Roger Is Dead," "The Old Soap Gourd," "The Tree in the Valley-O," "Two Dukes a' Riding," "Skin and Bones."

Reprinted in *Folk Songs of the Southern Appalachians* (second edition) © copyright 1997 University of Kentucky Press: "Among the Little White Daisies," "Bandyrowe," "Bangum Rid by the Riverside," "Dance to Your Daddy," "Darby's Ram," "The Death of the Robin," "Golden Ring Around the Susan Girl," "Killy Kranky," "London's Bridge," "Mama Told Me," "Old King Cole," "Skin and Bones."

"Epitaph for Myself" © copyright 1971 Jean Ritchie, Geordie Music.

Image Credits

ii, 7, 9, 15, 26 (both), 35, 36, 41, 49, 51, 55, 56, 57, 68, 77, 79, 88: Used by permission. Jean Ritchie and George Pickow collection (AFC 2008/005), American Folklife Center, Library of Congress.

v: Ritchie family collection. Used by permission.

x, xxiii, 6, 20, 104: Photo by Frank Hudson. Used by permission.

xii: Photo by Rae Russell. Used by permission. Jean Ritchie and George Pickow collection (AFC 2008/005), American Folklife Center, Library of Congress.

xviii–xix, 10: Jean Ritchie personal collection. Used by permission. Kentucky Educational Television.

xx: Photo by Beverly Fleming. Used by permission.

xxi: Used by permission of Berea College Hutchins Library, Department of Special Collections and Archives.

xxii, 31: Photo by George Pickow. Jean Ritchie personal collection. Used by permission.

3: Photo by George Pickow. Used by permission.

5, 17, 18: Photo by George Pickow. Used by permission. Jean Ritchie and George Pickow collection (AFC 2008/005), American Folklife Center, Library of Congress.

11, 21: Jean Ritchie personal collection. Used by permission.

19 (all): Photo by Velma Marcum. Used by permission.

25: Photo by George Pickow, Ritchie family collection. Used by permission.

29: Photo provided by Frank Hudson. Used by permission.

39: Photo courtesy of Joy Ritchie Powers. Used by permission.

38, 43, 45, 47, 61, 65, 71, 73, 75, 81, 83, 85, 87: Photo by George Pickow, for *The Swapping Song Book*, 1952. Reprinted by permission.

44: Painting by George Pickow; photo by Don Cardwell. Used by permission.

59, 62, 63 (both): Photo by Susan Brumfield. Berea, Kentucky, 2014.

67: Photo by Simon Smith. Used by permission.

Audio Recording Credits

"The Old Soup Gourd" by Jean Ritchie from the recording entitled *Children's Songs and Games from the Southern Mountains*, FW07054, courtesy of Smithsonian Folkways Recordings. ℗ © 1957. Used by permission.

"Kitty Alone" by Jean Ritchie from the recording entitled *Children's Songs and Games from the Southern Mountains*, FW07054, courtesy of Smithsonian Folkways Recordings. ℗ © 1957. Used by permission.

"Old Bangum" by Jean Ritchie from the recording entitled *British Traditional Ballads in the Southern Mountains, Volume 1*, FW02301, courtesy of Smithsonian Folkways Recordings. ℗ © 1960. Used by permission.

Notes on the Recordings

When Jean and I began working together on a collection of songs recalled from her childhood, we discussed the possibility of making a recording to accompany the anthology. We considered teaching the songs to children from Kentucky, or having Jean record them in a studio, but in those early stages of the project, we were more concerned with gathering songs for the book than making decisions about the CD that would eventually go along with it.

In November of 2007, during a visit to Jean and George's home in Port Washington, Jean made a "working" recording of some of the songs I hadn't yet transcribed. Jean's son Jon Pickow recorded Jean in their home studio as we talked informally about where and from whom she had learned them. As it turned out, those may have been among the last recordings made by Jean prior to her stroke.

After her move to Berea, Jean's health continued to improve. During a 2012 visit, I suggested that we finish *Kentucky Mother Goose*. She was enthusiastic about the project, and, after listening to the recording, she agreed to include it along with the book, even though it was not originally intended for that purpose.

As I resumed work on the manuscript, a very big question arose: What about recordings for the remaining songs? Though Jean had made remarkable progress, she was no longer performing publicly. After digging through old files, I found a "voice memo" that Jean and I had taped during a 2005 planning session for a workshop; we were preparing a presentation on children's game songs for a music teachers' conference in Texas. Four of the "missing" songs and games were part of that session, and my Texas Tech University colleague (and studio recording project genius) Will Strieder was able to salvage the memos and render them usable, if not exactly "studio quality." Also, Jean and George had traveled to Lubbock that year for a weekend of workshops and a "Tribute to Jean Ritchie" concert at Texas Tech. The concert featured faculty and student musicians singing and playing Jean's music for her and with her, as well as solo pieces by Jean herself. The live performance of "Jemmy Taylor-O" by Jean, myself, and the entire audience is among my own most cherished memories, and we included that track on the CD as well.

I knew Jean had recorded some of the songs commercially over the years, and I considered the possibility of a compilation to supplement the recordings from 2005 and 2007. (In fact, we filled out the CD with six tracks remastered from early LPs.) While doing research on one of the songs, though, I came across rare 1949 recordings of Jean made by folklorist Alan Lomax on the website of the Association for Cultural Equity. The ACE serves as "custodian" of the Alan Lomax Archive, which is described on its website as a "priceless collection of recorded music, dance, and the spoken word." In partnership with the American Folklife Center, and housed at the Library of Congress, the archive consists of "original recordings and photographs, media collections, library, manuscripts, and research materials assembled by Alan Lomax over the course of six decades, uniting them with the recordings made by Alan and his father, John Avery Lomax, for the Archive of American Folk Song from 1933 to 1942." The mission of the ACE is to preserve and disseminate Lomax's vast collections, and to "reconnect people and communities with their creative heritage."

Jean had met Alan Lomax shortly after she moved to New York City to become a social worker at the Henry Street Settlement School. After hearing her sing, Lomax asked her to record her family songs for the Library of Congress. The 1949 sessions took place in Lomax's apartment; in fact, his voice can be heard on several of the recordings. In these sessions (some of the earliest recordings of Jean Ritchie), Lomax was able to capture a large body of the Ritchie family repertoire, including hymns, ballads, play-parties and children's songs.

After a closer look at the digitized collection, I discovered twenty-one of Jean's *Kentucky Mother Goose* songs among those she had sung for Lomax. Nathan Salsburg, curator of the Alan Lomax Archive for the ACE, helped secure permission to include the rare recordings, copies of which have since been deposited in the sound archives of the Special Collections & Archives at the Hutchins Library at Berea College.

The notated songs in this book are not meant as direct transcriptions of the recordings on the CD. In some cases, Jean's written notes and print versions differ from various sung performances over the years, and the notation is intended as a composite rendition. For example, in play-party songs, such as "Built My Love a Fine Brick House," "Jemmy Taylor-O," and "Old King Cole," the verses are fairly consistent, but their order varies. In "Darby's Lamb (The Darby Ram)," "My Good Old Man," "Skin and Bones," and "Mammy Had an Old Goose," the plot of the story comes across, but some verses seem to be optional, and may or may not be sung. And Jean's versions of "Bandyrowe" and "Among the Little White Daisies" evolved to include verses about her own sons, Peter and Jon.

It's possible Jean occasionally chose to modify some lyrics for younger listeners when she recorded them on albums specifically for children. For example, this early Lomax field recording of "Mama Told Me (Old Shoe Boots)" is one of the few versions where the singer says of her suitor that she "wish't he was in hell!" after she "covered him well." In print and commercial recordings, she "covered him well, and he snored like the de'il." It's unlikely that this sort of editing was necessary in the family version, as it was understood that the text was tongue-in-cheek.

Detailed information for each sound recording is provided in the CD track listing.

CD Track Listing

1. "Churning Song" (0:51)
   Sung by Jean Ritchie. Interview with Susan Brumfield at the Ritchie–Pickow residence, Port Washington, New York. Recorded by Jon Pickow, November 2007.
2. "Darby's Lamb" (0:54)
   Sung by Jean Ritchie. Interview with Susan Brumfield at the Ritchie–Pickow residence, Port Washington, New York. Recorded by Jon Pickow, November 2007.
3. "Darby's Ram" (1:17)
   Sung by Jean Ritchie. From the Alan Lomax Collection at the American Folklife Center, Library of Congress. Used courtesy of the Association for Cultural Equity. Recorded by Alan Lomax, New York City, May 1949.
4. "God Bless the Moon" (0:44)
   Sung by Jean Ritchie. Interview with Susan Brumfield at the Ritchie–Pickow residence, Port Washington, New York. Recorded by Jon Pickow, November 2007.
5. "Hush, Little Baby" (0:43)
   Sung by Jean Ritchie. Interview with Susan Brumfield at the Ritchie–Pickow residence, Port Washington, New York. Recorded by Jon Pickow, November 2007.
6. "Swing-a-Swong" (0:36)
   Sung by Jean Ritchie. Interview with Susan Brumfield at the Ritchie–Pickow residence, Port Washington, New York. Recorded by Jon Pickow, November 2007.
7. "A Man of Words and Not of Deeds" (0:34)
   Spoken by Jean Ritchie. Interview with Susan Brumfield at the Ritchie–Pickow residence, Port Washington, New York. Recorded by Susan Brumfield, July 2005.
8. "Froggy in the Meadow" (1:18)
   Spoken by Jean Ritchie. Interview with Susan Brumfield at the Ritchie–Pickow residence, Port Washington, New York. Recorded by Susan Brumfield, July 2005.

9. "Jaybird, Jaybird, Sittin' on a Limb" (0:22)
   Spoken by Jean Ritchie. Interview with Susan Brumfield at the Ritchie–Pickow residence, Port Washington, New York. Recorded by Susan Brumfield, July 2005.
10. "Take It Off or Knock It Off" (3:36)
   Spoken by Jean Ritchie. Interview with Susan Brumfield at the Ritchie–Pickow residence, Port Washington, New York. Recorded by Susan Brumfield, July 2005.
11. "William Tremmytoe" (0:28)
   Sung by Jean Ritchie. From the Alan Lomax Collection at the American Folklife Center, Library of Congress. Used courtesy of the Association for Cultural Equity. Recorded by Alan Lomax, New York City, May 1949.
12. "Among the Little White Daisies" (1:09)
   Sung by Jean Ritchie. From the Alan Lomax Collection at the American Folklife Center, Library of Congress. Used courtesy of the Association for Cultural Equity. Recorded by Alan Lomax, New York City, May 1949.
13. "Chick-to-ma, Chick-to-ma Cranie Crow" (1:38)
   Spoken by Jean Ritchie. Interview with Susan Brumfield at the Ritchie–Pickow residence, Port Washington, New York. Recorded by Jon Pickow, November 2007.
14. "Go In and Out the Window" (0:58)
   Sung by Jean Ritchie. From the Alan Lomax Collection at the American Folklife Center, Library of Congress. Used courtesy of the Association for Cultural Equity. Recorded by Alan Lomax, New York City, June 1949.
15. "Golden Ring Around the Susan Girl" (0:32)
   Sung by Jean Ritchie. From the Alan Lomax Collection at the American Folklife Center, Library of Congress. Used courtesy of the Association for Cultural Equity. Recorded by Alan Lomax, New York City, May 1949.
16. "Golden Ring Around the Susan Girl" (2) (1:38)
   Written and performed by Jean Ritchie. Published by Geordie Music Publishing (ASCAP). Produced under license from Warner Bros. Records Inc. ISRC: USWB10400524.
17. "Green Gravel" (1:12)
   Sung by Jean Ritchie. Interview with Susan Brumfield at the Ritchie–Pickow residence, Port Washington, New York. Recorded by Jon Pickow, November 2007.
18. "Jenny, Put Your Kettle On" (0:24)
   Sung by Jean Ritchie. From the Alan Lomax Collection at the American Folklife Center, Library of Congress. Used courtesy of the Association for Cultural Equity. Recorded by Alan Lomax, New York City, May 1949.
19. "King William" (1:06)
   Sung by Jean Ritchie. Interview with Susan Brumfield at the Ritchie–Pickow residence, Port Washington, New York. Recorded by Jon Pickow, November 2007.

20. "London's Bridge" (1:46)

    Sung by Jean Ritchie. Interview with Susan Brumfield at the Ritchie–Pickow residence, Port Washington, New York. Recorded by Jon Pickow, November 2007.

21. "Mommy, Mommy, I Am Sick" (0:47)

    Sung by Jean Ritchie. Interview with Susan Brumfield at the Ritchie–Pickow residence, Port Washington, New York. Recorded by Jon Pickow, November 2007.

22. "Mommy, Mommy, I Am Sick" (2) (1:11)

    Sung by Jean Ritchie. Used by permission, Berea College Hutchins Library Department of Special Collections. Celebration of Traditional Music, October 28, 1993.

23. "Old Roger Is Dead" (1:15)

    Sung by Jean Ritchie. From the Alan Lomax Collection at the American Folklife Center, Library of Congress. Used courtesy of the Association for Cultural Equity. Recorded by Alan Lomax, New York City, May 1949.

24. "Poor Little Kitty Puss" (0:25)

    Sung by Jean Ritchie. Interview with Susan Brumfield at the Ritchie–Pickow residence, Port Washington, New York. Recorded by Jon Pickow, November 2007.

25. "The Old Soap Gourd" (1:06)

    Sung by Jean Ritchie. From *Jean Ritchie Sings Children's Songs and Games from the Southern Mountains.* Smithsonian Folkways FW07053_109, 1957.

26. "Two Dukes A-Rovin'" (2:27)

    Sung by Jean Ritchie. Interview with Susan Brumfield at the Ritchie–Pickow residence, Port Washington, New York. Recorded by Jon Pickow, November 2007.

27. "Who Killed Cock Robin?" (0:49)

    Sung by Jean Ritchie. Interview with Susan Brumfield at the Ritchie–Pickow residence, Port Washington, New York. Recorded by Jon Pickow, November 2007.

28. "Kitty Alone (Bandyrowe)" (2:24)

    Sung by Jean Ritchie. From *Jean Ritchie Sings Children's Songs and Games from the Southern Mountains.* Smithsonian Folkways FW07053_109, 1957.

29. "Old Bangum (Bangum Rid by the Riverside)" (2:00)

    Sung by Jean Ritchie. From *British Traditional Ballads in the Southern Mountains, Vol. 1.* Smithsonian Folkways FW02301 / FA 1960.

30. "Big Glass Doll" (1:38)

    Sung by Jean Ritchie. Interview with Susan Brumfield at the Ritchie–Pickow residence, Port Washington, New York. Recorded by Jon Pickow, November 2007.

31. "Big Glass Doll" (2) (1:31)

    Sung by Jean Ritchie. From the Alan Lomax Collection at the American Folklife Center, Library of Congress. Used courtesy of the Association for Cultural Equity. Recorded by Alan Lomax, New York City, May 1949.

32. "Cedar Swamp" ("Built My Love a Big Fine House") (1:19)
    Written and performed by Jean Ritchie. Published by Geordie Music Publishing (ASCAP). Produced under license from Elektra Entertainment Group Inc. ISRC: USEE10412236.
33. "Dance to Your Daddy" (1:03)
    Sung by Jean Ritchie. Interview with Susan Brumfield at the Ritchie–Pickow residence, Port Washington, New York. Recorded by Jon Pickow, November 2007.
34. "Dance to Your Daddy" (2) (0:18)
    Sung by Jean Ritchie. From the Alan Lomax Collection at the American Folklife Center, Library of Congress. Used courtesy of the Association for Cultural Equity. Recorded by Alan Lomax, New York City, May 1949.
35. "Jemmy Taylor-O" (0:27)
    Sung by Jean Ritchie. From the Alan Lomax Collection at the American Folklife Center, Library of Congress. Used courtesy of the Association for Cultural Equity. Recorded by Alan Lomax, New York City, May 1949.
36. "Jemmy Taylor-O" (2) (2:03)
    Sung by Jean Ritchie and Susan Brumfield, with "Last Night's Fun" and "The Sweet Peas." "A Tribute to Jean Ritchie" concert, Texas Tech University, Lubbock, Texas. Recorded by Will Strieder, October 8, 2005.
37. "Killy Kranky" (1:05)
    Written and performed by Jean Ritchie. Published by Geordie Music Publishing (ASCAP). Produced under license from Elektra Entertainment Group Inc. ISRC: USEE10412243.
38. "Mama Told Me (Old Shoe Boots)" (1:17)
    Sung by Jean Ritchie. From the Alan Lomax Collection at the American Folklife Center, Library of Congress. Used courtesy of the Association for Cultural Equity. Recorded by Alan Lomax, Edinburgh, Scotland, November 1953.
39. "Mammy Had an Old Goose" (1:32)
    Sung by Jean Ritchie. Interview with Susan Brumfield at the Ritchie–Pickow residence, Port Washington, New York. Recorded by Jon Pickow, November 2007.
40. "Mammy Had an Old Goose" (2) (1:56)
    Sung by Jean Ritchie. From the Alan Lomax Collection at the American Folklife Center, Library of Congress. Used courtesy of the Association for Cultural Equity. Recorded by Alan Lomax, New York City, June 1949.
41. "My Good Old Man" (1:50)
    Sung by Jean Ritchie. Interview with Susan Brumfield at the Ritchie–Pickow residence, Port Washington, New York. Recorded by Jon Pickow, November 2007.

42. "My Good Old Man" (2) (2:24)
    Sung by Jean Ritchie. From the Alan Lomax Collection at the American Folklife Center, Library of Congress. Used courtesy of the Association for Cultural Equity. Recorded by Alan Lomax, New York City, May 1949.
43. "Old Daddy Grumble" (2:23)
    Sung by Jean Ritchie. From the Alan Lomax Collection at the American Folklife Center, Library of Congress. Used courtesy of the Association for Cultural Equity. Recorded by Alan Lomax, New York City, March 1949.
44. "Old King Cole Was a Jolly Old Soul" (0:58)
    Sung by Jean Ritchie. From the Alan Lomax Collection at the American Folklife Center, Library of Congress. Used courtesy of the Association for Cultural Equity. Recorded by Alan Lomax, New York City, May 1949.
45. "Old King Quine" (0:30)
    Sung by Jean Ritchie. Interview with Susan Brumfield at the Ritchie–Pickow residence, Port Washington, New York. Recorded by Jon Pickow, November 2007.
46. "Skin and Bones" (1:19)
    Sung by Jean Ritchie. From the Alan Lomax Collection at the American Folklife Center, Library of Congress. Used courtesy of the Association for Cultural Equity. Recorded by Alan Lomax, New York City, May 1949.
47. "Soldier, Soldier" (1:02)
    Sung by Jean Ritchie. Interview with Susan Brumfield at the Ritchie–Pickow residence, Port Washington, New York. Recorded by Jon Pickow, November 2007.
48. "The Hunting Tale" (0:45)
    Sung by Jean Ritchie. Interview with Susan Brumfield at the Ritchie–Pickow residence, Port Washington, New York. Recorded by Jon Pickow, November 2007.
49. "The Tree in the Valley-O" (2:04)
    Sung by Jean Ritchie. From the Alan Lomax Collection at the American Folklife Center, Library of Congress. Used courtesy of the Association for Cultural Equity. Recorded by Alan Lomax, New York City, May 1949.
50. "Where Are You Going, Little Birdie?" (1:37)
    Sung by Jean Ritchie. Interview with Susan Brumfield at the Ritchie–Pickow residence, Port Washington, New York. Recorded by Jon Pickow, November 2007.

Harp on the willow tree,
Now it is hung.
One man, one faith, one God;
To them I clung.
Sweet were the songs of life,
Now they are sung.
Harp on the willow tree,
Now it is hung.

Dear little son of mine,
Child on your knee.
Sing him your songs of life,
Let him fly free.
Dear little son of mine,
Child on your knee.
Sing them for you, for him,
Sing them for me.

Jean Ritchie, "Epitaph for Myself" ("Songs of Life")